Speeches

THAT MADE HISTORY

Speeches
THAT MADE HISTORY

CASSELL
ILLUSTRATED

An Hachette UK Company
www.hachette.co.uk

First published in Great Britain in 2018 by Cassell, a division of
Octopus Publishing Group Ltd
Carmelite House
50 Victoria Embankment
London EC4Y 0DZ
www.octopusbooks.co.uk

ISBN 978-0-7537-3293-9

A CIP catalogue record for this book is available from the British Library

Printed and bound in China

10 9 8 7 6 5 4 3 2 1

Publisher: Lucy Pessell
Editor: Sarah Vaughan
Designer: Lisa Laton
Production Controller: Sarah Kulasek-Boyd

CONTENTS

INTRODUCTION

For many thousands of years, people have used oratory to influence others, but what exactly makes a speech great? Is it the choice of words, the feelings they express, the passion with which the speaker delivers them, the circumstances or the lasting effect that the speech has on what other people think or do, or even on the course of history? In fact, it can be all or any of these.

The earliest speeches that we know have, ironically, survived only because they were written down afterwards. Although they would have been heard by only a few people at the time, their influence has spread. For example, just a few soldiers would have heard Julius Caesar mutter *'Alea iacta est'* ('The die is cast') as he defied the Roman Senate and crossed the Rubicon into Italy with an army at his back, but that step has influenced the whole of Western history for more than 2,000 years.

The advent of mass media has had a profound effect on the influence of the spoken word: politicians are no longer trying to inspire a few people in a room, they are addressing millions via radio, television or the internet, as well as posterity.
The speeches in *Speeches that Made History* are divided into ten categories: Ancient History, Love, Religion, Science, Patriotism, Philosophy, Humanity & Liberty, Sport, Politics and War.
The speeches in Ancient History, Patriotism, Politics and War inspired people to act, while those in Love, Religion, Science, Philosophy, Humanity & Liberty and Sport have primarily changed the way people think or look at the world.

As well as formal speeches, many announcements and off-the-cuff remarks have also been included, because whether poignant in today's society like Warhol's 'In the future, everybody will be world famous for 15 minutes', the announcement of Princess Diana's death, or the proclamation of a scientific breakthrough like Newton's equation for the Universal Law of Gravitation, they all have chronicled our history.

ANCIENT HISTORY

"MERNEPTAH FIRST REFERENCES ISRAEL"
Pharoah Merneptah

Merneptah, the thirteenth son of Ramesses II, succeeded to his father's throne at the age of 60. Relatively little is known about his nine-year reign, except from inscriptions at his mortuary temple concerning his military campaigns against the Libyans and the rebellious 'Asiatics' of various nations. This first reference to the people of Israel makes it clear that at this stage they did not have a settled home: while Ashkelon, Gezer and Yanoam have the hieroglyphs indicating a foreign city-state and people, Israel is indicated as a foreign people only. The 125-inch black granite stele was found by the British archaeologist Flinders Petrie in 1896 and it is now in the Egyptian Museum in Cairo.

The princes are prostrate, saying 'Shalom'!
Not one is raising his head among the Nine Bows.
Now that Libya [Tehenu] has come to ruin,
Hatti is pacified.
The Canaan has been plundered into every sort of woe;
Ashkelon has been overcome;
Gezer has been captured;

Yanoam is made nonexistent;
Israel is laid waste and his seed is not;
Hurru is become a widow because of Egypt

"PLATO'S THRASYMACHUS IN *THE REPUBLIC*"
Plato

Among Plato's most important works is *The Republic*, which
was written in c. 380 BCE. It is one of his Socratic dialogues
– fictionalized accounts of discussions between Greek
philosophers – although it is probable that the ideas mentioned
reflect those of the protagonists. In a discussion on the nature
of justice, and on whether the just man is happier than the
unjust man, he has the Chalcedonian philosopher Thrasymachus
say that justice is not about right or wrong, but is in the interest
of those in power. In the dialogue, Sophocles proves this
definition wrong. The modern equivalent could be said to be
'Might is right'.

I proclaim that justice is nothing else than the interest of the
stronger.

"A PYRRHIC VICTORY"
King Pyrrhus of Epirus

By the early 3rd century BCE Rome had expanded her territory to a large part of the Italian peninsula but then, after a minor skirmish in 281 BCE with Tarentum – one of the Greek colonies in southern Italy – first came into conflict with the Greeks, led by Pyrrhus. The Greeks and their allies won a series of battles at Heraclea (280 BCE), Asculum (279 BCE) and then at Beneventum (275 BCE),but with such great losses that the Greeks were eventually forced to admit that they could no longer protect their overseas colonies in the region and the term Pyrrhic victory came to mean a victory not worth the cost.

If we are victorious in one more battle with the Romans, we shall be utterly ruined.

"THE CODE OF HAMMURABI"
Hammurabi (King of Babylon)

Hammurabi was the sixth king of the Amorite dynasty, who expanded a small city-state into a large empire during his long reign. Although fragments had been known about for many years, the stele containing a long prologue describing the king's achievements and 282 provisions – The Code of Hammurabi – was discovered in 1901 in the Elamite city of Susa. The 2.2 m (7 ft 5 in) black diorite stele is now in the Louvre in Paris. The laws are chiefly about family life, property and trade but provide a great deal of detail about life in ancient Babylonia.

If a man, in a case pending judgement, has uttered threats against the witnesses, or has not justified the word that he has spoken, if that case be a capital suit, that man shall be put to death.

If he has offered corn or money to the witnesses, he shall himself bear the sentence of that case.

If a man has stolen the goods of temple or palace, that man shall be killed, and he who has received the stolen thing from his hand shall be put to death.

If a man has stolen ox or sheep or ass, or pig, or ship, whether from the temple or the palace, he shall pay thirtyfold.

If he be a poor man, he shall render tenfold.

If the thief has nought to pay, he shall be put to death.

If a man has stolen the son of a freeman, he shall be put to death.

If a man has captured either a manservant or a maidservant, a fugitive, in the open country and has driven him back to his master, the owner of the slave shall pay him two shekels of silver.

If either a governor or a magistrate has taken to himself the men of the levy, or has accepted and sent on the king's errand a hired substitute, that governor or magistrate shall be put to death.

A votary, merchant, or foreign sojourner may sell his field, his garden, or his house; the buyer shall carry on the business of the field, garden, or house which he has bought.

If a man has taken a field to cultivate and has not caused the corn to grow in the field, and has not done the entrusted work on the field, one shall put him to account and he shall give corn like its neighbour.

If he has not cultivated the field and has left it to itself, he shall give corn like its neighbour to the owner of the field, and the field he left he shall break up with hoes and shall harrow it and return to the owner of the field.

If a man has given his field for produce to a cultivator, and has received the produce of his field, and afterwards a thunderstorm has ravaged the field or carried away the produce, the loss is the cultivator's.

If a man has neglected to strengthen his bank of the canal, has not strengthened his bank, a breach has opened out itself in his bank, and the waters have carried away the meadow, the man in whose bank the breach has been opened shall render back the corn which he has caused to be lost.

If a man without the consent of the owner of the orchard has cut down a tree in a man's orchard, he shall pay half a mina of silver.

If an agent has taken money from a merchant and his merchant has disputed with him, that merchant shall put the agent to account before God and witnesses concerning the money taken, and the agent shall give to the merchant the money as much as he has taken threefold.

If a wine merchant has collected a riotous assembly in her house and has not seized those rioters and driven them to the palace, that wine merchant shall be put to death.

If a votary, a lady, who is not living in the convent, has opened a wine shop or has entered a wine shop for drink, that woman one shall burn her.

If the wife of a man has been caught in lying with another male, one shall bind them and throw them into the waters.

If the owner of the wife would save his wife or the king would save his servant (he may).

If a man has forced the wife of a man who has not known the male and is dwelling in the house of her father, and has lain in her bosom and one has caught him, that man shall be killed, the woman herself shall go free.

If the wife of a man her husband has accused her, and she has not been caught in lying with another male, she shall swear by God and shall return to her house.

If a man has put away his bride who has not borne him children, he shall give her money as much as her dowry, and shall pay her the marriage portion which she brought from her father's house, and shall put her away.

If a woman hates her husband and has said 'Thou shalt not possess me', one shall enquire into her past what is her lack, and if she has been economical and has no vice, and her husband has gone out and greatly belittled her, that woman has no blame, she shall take her marriage portion and go off to her father's house.

If she has not been economical, a goer about, has wasted her house, has belittled her husband, that woman one shall throw her into the waters.

If a man's wife on account of another male has caused her husband to be killed, that woman upon a stake one shall set her.

If a man has married a wife and she has borne him children, and that woman has gone to her fate, her father shall have no claim on her marriage portion, her marriage portion is her children's forsooth.

If a man has married a wife, and she has not granted him children, that woman has gone to her fate, if his father-in-law has returned him the dowry that that man brought to the house of his father-in-law, her husband shall have no claim on the marriage portion of that woman, her marriage portion belongs to the house of her father forsooth.

If a man has set his face to cut off his son, has said to the judge 'I will cut off my son,' the judge shall enquire into his reasons, and if the son has not committed a heavy crime which cuts off from sonship, the father shall not cut off his son from sonship.

If he has committed against his father a heavy crime which cuts off from sonship, for the first time the judge shall bring back his face; if he has committed a heavy crime for the second time, the father shall cut off his son from sonship.

If a son of a palace warder, or of a vowed woman, has known his father's house, and has hated the father that brought him up or the mother that brought him up, and has gone off to the house of his father, one shall tear out his eye.

If a man has caused the loss of a gentleman's eye, his eye one shall cause to be lost.

If he has shattered a gentleman's limb, one shall shatter his limb.

If a man has made the tooth of a man that is his equal to fall out, one shall make his tooth fall out.

If a man has struck a gentleman's daughter and caused her to drop what is in her womb, he shall pay ten shekels of silver for what was in her womb.

If that woman has died, one shall put to death his daughter.

If the daughter of a poor man through his blows he has caused to drop that which is in her womb, he shall pay five shekels of silver.

If that woman has died, he shall pay half a mina of silver.

If he has struck a gentleman's maidservant and caused her to drop that which is in her womb, he shall pay two shekels of silver.

If that maidservant has died, he shall pay one-third of a mina of silver.

If a man has hired an ox and through neglect or by blows has caused it to die, ox for ox to the owner of the ox he shall render.

If a man has hired an ox, and God has struck it and it has died, the man who has hired the ox shall swear before God and shall go free.

If a shepherd to whom cows and sheep have been given him to breed, has falsified and changed their price, or has sold them, one shall put him to account, and he shall render cows and sheep to their owner tenfold what he has stolen.

If in a sheepfold a stroke of God has taken place or a lion has killed, the shepherd shall purge himself before God, and the accident to the fold the owner of the fold shall face it.

If a shepherd has been careless and in a sheepfold caused a loss to take place, the shepherd shall make good the fault of the loss which he has caused to be in the fold and shall pay cows or sheep and shall give to their owner.

If a man has bought a manservant or a maidservant and has a complaint, his seller shall answer the complaint.

If they are natives of another land the buyer shall tell out before God the money he paid, and the owner of the manservant or the maidservant shall give to the merchant the money he paid, and shall recover his manservant or his maidservant.

"ADVICE TO CROESUS OF LYDIA"
The Delphic Oracle

In ancient Greece, people consulted oracles to help them make important decisions. At Delphi, where an oracle was in operation for hundreds of years, the oracles were delivered by a priestess known as the Pythia, from a cave above a deep fissure that may have been filled with trance-inducing gases expelled from the geological fault below. Answers from the Pythia were notoriously ambiguous, none more so than that given to Croesus of Lydia (born 595 BCE, reigned c. 560–547 BCE), who consulted various oracles as to whether he should pursue his military campaign against the Persians. He took her answer to mean that the Persian empire would fall, but instead lost his own.

If Croesus attacks the Persians, he will destroy a great empire.

LOVE

"A QUEEN OF PEOPLE'S HEARTS"
Diana, Princess of Wales

Towards the end of his interview with Princess Diana, journalist
Martin Bashir moves on to her future and asks whether she
thinks she will ever be Queen. She replies, 'No', and when
asked why, gives the answer below. Given the damage that
her behaviour had done to the royal family's image, it is –
with hindsight – not surprising that some members of the
establishment might have regarded the possibility of her
becoming Queen with some alarm. The interview led to
increased sympathy for the princess, who was by now very
skilled in dealing with the media and knew just how to get
her point across. The enormous sympathy that the interview
engendered in her millions of fans, and in the tabloid press in
particular, made it obvious that she had no intention of quietly
fading into the background.

I'd like to be a queen of people's hearts, in people's hearts, but I
don't see myself being Queen of this country. I don't think many
people will want me to be Queen. Actually, when I say many
people I mean the establishment that I married into, because they
have decided that I'm a non-starter.

"FROM *DE DILIGENDO DEO (ON THE LOVE OF GOD)*"
Saint Bernard of Clairvaux

A Cistercian abbot, and very conservative, Saint Bernard of Clairvaux was one of the leading theologians of the 12th century. For a period he was more influential than the popes of the day. Under his leadership, Cistercian monasticism – with its emphasis on poverty, abstinence and prayer – spread far and wide across northwestern Europe. He was instrumental in suppressing the Cathar and Waldensian heresies, in sorting out the unholy mess of the schism of 1130–1138 when there were two rival popes, in promoting the cult of the Virgin Mary and in encouraging the Second Crusade to the Holy Land. His most important work was *De Diligendo Deo (On the Love of God)*, but the line below – meaning that to be with me you must put up with the things about me that you don't like – has passed into more common knowledge.

Qui me amat, amat et canem meum. (Love me, love my dog.)

"*ECLOGUE X – GALLUS*"
Virgil

Virgil is widely regarded as one of the best Roman poets of the era after the death of Julius Caesar. The first of his major works, the *Eclogues* (or *Bucolicae*) were written to be performed on the stage. They contain a heady mixture of eroticism and Virgil's own political vision and are chiefly set in the countryside and feature shepherds. The tenth Eclogue is the passionate last oration of the poet Gaius Cornelius Gallus in Arcadia. He envisages his friend dying of love in a beautiful landscape, and thus started the pastoral tradition in Western arts and literature.

ECLOGUE X – GALLUS

This now, the very latest of my toils,
Vouchsafe me, Arethusa! needs must I
Sing a brief song to Gallus- brief, but yet
Such as Lycoris' self may fitly read.
Who would not sing for Gallus? So, when thou
Beneath Sicanian billows glidest on,
May Doris blend no bitter wave with thine,
Begin! The love of Gallus be our theme,
And the shrewd pangs he suffered, while, hard by,
The flat-nosed she-goats browse the tender brush.
We sing not to deaf ears; no word of ours
But the woods echo it. What groves or lawns
Held you, ye Dryad-maidens, when for love-
Love all unworthy of a loss so dear-
Gallus lay dying? for neither did the slopes
Of Pindus or Parnassus stay you then,
No, nor Aonian Aganippe. Him
Even the laurels and the tamarisks wept;
For him, outstretched beneath a lonely rock,

Wept pine-clad Maenalus, and the flinty crags
Of cold Lycaeus. The sheep too stood around-
Of us they feel no shame, poet divine;
Nor of the flock be thou ashamed: even fair
Adonis by the rivers fed his sheep-
Came shepherd too, and swine-herd footing slow,
And, from the winter-acorns dripping-wet
Menalcas. All with one accord exclaim:
"From whence this love of thine?" Apollo came;
"Gallus, art mad?" he cried, "thy bosom's care
Another love is following." Therewithal
Silvanus came, with rural honours crowned;
The flowering fennels and tall lilies shook
Before him. Yea, and our own eyes beheld
Pan, god of Arcady, with blood-red juice
Of the elder-berry, and with vermilion, dyed.
"Wilt ever make an end?" quoth he, "behold
Love recks not aught of it: his heart no more
With tears is sated than with streams the grass,
Bees with the cytisus, or goats with leaves."
"Yet will ye sing, Arcadians, of my woes
Upon your mountains," sadly he replied-
"Arcadians, that alone have skill to sing.
O then how softly would my ashes rest,
If of my love, one day, your flutes should tell!
And would that I, of your own fellowship,
Or dresser of the ripening grape had been,
Or guardian of the flock! for surely then,
Let Phyllis, or Amyntas, or who else,
Bewitch me- what if swart Amyntas be?
Dark is the violet, dark the hyacinth-
Among the willows, 'neath the limber vine,
Reclining would my love have lain with me,
Phyllis plucked garlands, or Amyntas sung.
Here are cool springs, soft mead and grove, Lycoris;
Here might our lives with time have worn away.
But me mad love of the stern war-god holds
Armed amid weapons and opposing foes.

Whilst thou- Ah! might I but believe it not!-
Alone without me, and from home afar,
Look'st upon Alpine snows and frozen Rhine.
Ah! may the frost not hurt thee, may the sharp
And jagged ice not wound thy tender feet!
I will depart, re-tune the songs I framed
In verse Chalcidian to the oaten reed
Of the Sicilian swain. Resolved am I
In the woods, rather, with wild beasts to couch,
And bear my doom, and character my love
Upon the tender tree-trunks: they will grow,
And you, my love, grow with them. And meanwhile
I with the Nymphs will haunt Mount Maenalus,
Or hunt the keen wild boar. No frost so cold
But I will hem with hounds thy forest-glades,
Parthenius. Even now, methinks, I range
O'er rocks, through echoing groves, and joy to launch
Cydonian arrows from a Parthian bow.-
As if my madness could find healing thus,
Or that god soften at a mortal's grief!
Now neither Hamadryads, no, nor songs
Delight me more: ye woods, away with you!
No pangs of ours can change him; not though we
In the mid-frost should drink of Hebrus' stream,
And in wet winters face Sithonian snows,
Or, when the bark of the tall elm-tree bole
Of drought is dying, should, under Cancer's Sign,
In Aethiopian deserts drive our flocks.
Love conquers all things; yield we too to love!"

These songs, Pierian Maids, shall it suffice
Your poet to have sung, the while he sat,
And of slim mallow wove a basket fine:
To Gallus ye will magnify their worth,
Gallus, for whom my love grows hour by hour,
As the green alder shoots in early Spring.
Come, let us rise: the shade is wont to be
Baneful to singers; baneful is the shade

Cast by the juniper, crops sicken too
In shade. Now homeward, having fed your fill-
Eve's star is rising-go, my she-goats, go.

RELIGION

"GOD HAS GIVEN US INTELLECT"
Galileo Galilei

The Italian astronomer Galileo Galilei was one of the first to construct a telescope and use it to study the heavens. In 1610, he discovered that the planet Jupiter had four satellites orbiting around it like the Moon does around the Earth, and that the planet Venus has a full phase, again, like the Moon. The former observation contradicted the Aristotelian Earth-centred model of the cosmos, in which all other astronomical bodies orbit the Earth, and the latter the Ptolemaic theory that Venus always remains between the Earth and the Sun (if this were so, the planet would never show as a full disc). Both ideas were contrary to Church teachings and Galileo – a deeply religious man – faced accusations of heresy. The reflection that God wouldn't have given us brains if he hadn't meant us to use them is an early defence of Francis Bacon's evidence-based scientific method.

. . . I do not feel obliged to believe that the same God who has endowed us with senses, reason and intellect has intended to forgo their use and by some other means to give us knowledge which we can attain by them.

"SEARCH FOR THE YOUNG CHILD, THE KING OF THE JEWS"
King Herod (Herod the Great)

Herod I – also known as Herod the Great – was a Roman client king of Judaea. In Chapter II of St Matthew's Gospel, he is visited by the three wise men, who inform him that they are looking for the newly born King of the Jews. As he is currently holder of that position, he calls together the most important priests and scribes, who tell him that the prophet [Micah] has written that the King of the Jews will be born in Bethlehem. Herod sends the wise men to Bethlehem with the instruction to murder the child when he is found. When the wise men do not return, Herod sends his troops to slaughter all of the children in the city under the age of two.

Go and search diligently for the young child; and when ye have found him, bring me word again, that I may come and worship him also.

"PHILOSOPHY BRINGETH MEN'S MIND BACK TO RELIGION"
Francis Bacon

Philosopher, statesman, scientist and author, Francis Bacon
is chiefly remembered today for overturning the method of
scientific investigation developed by Aristotle – that if sufficiently
clever men debated a problem for long enough they would
get the right answer – in favour of empirical observation of a
phenomenon or object leading to a discovery of the facts about
it. In a time when there was increasing concern about the
possible risks of atheism to society, his observations led him to
conclude that there had to be a creator as no other explanation
fitted what he saw.

I had rather believe all the fables in the Legend, and the Talmud,
and the Alcoran, than that this universal frame is without a
mind. And therefore, God never wrought miracle, to convince
atheism, because his ordinary works convince it. It is true, that
a little philosophy inclineth man's mind to atheism; but depth
in philosophy bringeth men's minds about to religion. For while
the mind of man looketh upon second causes scattered, it may
sometimes rest in them, and go no further; but when it beholdeth
the chain of them, confederate and linked together, it must needs
fly to Providence and Deity. Nay, even that school which is most
accused of atheism doth most demonstrate religion; that is, the
school of Leucippus and Democritus and Epicurus. For it is a
thousand times more credible, that four mutable elements, and
one immutable fifth essence, duly and eternally placed, need
no God, than that an army of infinite small portions, or seeds
unplaced, should have produced this order and beauty, without a
divine marshal. The Scripture saith, The fool hath said in his heart,
there is no God; it is not said, The fool hath thought in his heart; so
as he rather saith it, by rote to himself, as that he would have,

than that he can thoroughly believe it, or be persuaded of it. For none deny, there is a God, but those for whom it maketh that there were no God. It appeareth in nothing more, that atheism is rather in the lip, than in the heart of man, than by this; that atheists will ever be talking of that their opinion, as if they fainted in it, within themselves, and would be glad to be strengthened, by the consent of others . . . The causes of atheism are: divisions in religion, if they be many; for any one main division, addeth zeal to both sides; but many divisions introduce atheism. Another is, scandal of priests; when it is come to that which St Bernard saith . . . A third is, custom of profane scoffing in holy matters; which doth, by little and little, deface the reverence of religion. And lastly, learned times, specially with peace and prosperity; for troubles and adversities do more bow men's minds to religion. They that deny a God, destroy man's nobility; for certainly man is of kin to the beasts, by his body; and, if he be not of kin to God, by his spirit, he is a base and ignoble creature. It destroys likewise magnanimity, and the raising of human nature; for take an example of a dog, and mark what a generosity and courage he will put on, when he finds himself maintained by a man; who to him is instead of a God; which courage is manifestly such, as that creature, without that confidence of a better nature than his own, could never attain. So man, when he resteth and assureth himself, upon divine protection and favour, gathered a force and faith, which human nature in itself could not obtain. Therefore, as atheism is in all respects hateful, so in this, that it depriveth human nature of the means to exalt itself, above human frailty. As it is in particular persons, so it is in nations. Never was there such a state for magnanimity as Rome. Of this state hear what Cicero saith: Pride ourselves as we may upon our country, yet are we not in number superior to the Spaniards, nor in strength to the Gauls, nor in cunning to the Carthaginians, not to the Greeks in arts, nor to the Italians and Latins themselves in the homely and native sense which belongs to his nation and land; it is in piety only and religion, and the wisdom of regarding the providence of the immortal gods as that which rules and governs all things, that we have surpassed all nations and peoples.

"THE FIRE SERMON"
Buddha

The son of the ruler of Kapilavastu, Siddhartha Gautama became the leader of one of the most widespread and popular religions in the world. He gave up his privileged position and became an ascetic, nomadic beggar, fasting and meditating in order to achieve enlightenment. In the Pali tradition, his third teaching after he gained enlightenment was the Adittapariyaya Sutta – the Fire Sermon, which he preached to 1,000 newly converted ascetics who had formerly been fire worshippers. The teaching shows them that in order to achieve enlightenment, they must learn to divorce themselves from their senses and the mental processes that accompany them.

Thus I heard. On one occasion the Blessed One was living at Gaya, at Gayasisa, together with a thousand bhikkhus. There he addressed the bhikkhus.

Bhikkhus, all is burning. And what is the all that is burning?

The eye is burning, forms are burning, eye-consciousness is burning, eye-contact is burning, also whatever is felt as pleasant or painful or neither-painful-nor-pleasant that arises with eye-contact for its indispensable condition, that too is burning. Burning with what? Burning with the fire of lust, with the fire of hate, with the fire of delusion. I say it is burning with birth, aging and death, with sorrows, with lamentations, with pains, with griefs, with despairs.

The ear is burning, sounds are burning . . .

The nose is burning, odours are burning . . .

The tongue is burning, flavours are burning . . .

The body is burning, tangibles are burning . . .

The mind is burning, ideas are burning, mind-consciousness is burning, mind-contact is burning, also whatever is felt as pleasant or painful or neither-painful-nor-pleasant that arises with mind-contact for its indispensable condition, that too is burning.

Burning with what? Burning with the fire of lust, with the fire of hate, with the fire of delusion. I say it is burning with birth, aging and death, with sorrows, with lamentations, with pains, with griefs, with despairs.

Bhikkhus, when a noble follower who has heard (the truth) sees thus, he finds estrangement in the eye, finds estrangement in forms, finds estrangement in eye-consciousness, finds estrangement in eye-contact, and whatever is felt as pleasant or painful or neither painful-nor-pleasant that arises with eye-contact for its indispensable condition, in that too he finds estrangement.

He finds estrangement in the ear . . . in sounds . . .

He finds estrangement in the nose . . . in odours . . .

He finds estrangement in the tongue . . . in flavours . . .

He finds estrangement in the body . . . in tangibles . . .

He finds estrangement in the mind, finds estrangement in ideas, finds estrangement in mind-consciousness, finds estrangement in mind-contact, and whatever is felt as pleasant or painful or neither-painful-nor-pleasant that arises with mind-contact for its indispensable condition, in that too he finds estrangement.

When he finds estrangement, passion fades out. With the fading of passion, he is liberated. When liberated, there is knowledge that he is liberated. He understands: 'Birth is exhausted, the holy life has been lived out, what can be done is done, of this there is no more beyond.'

"THE LORD'S PRAYER"
Jesus Christ

In chapters 5–7 of St Matthew's Gospel – the passage known
as the Sermon on the Mount – Christ expresses many of what
would become the most important ideas of Christianity,
including the spiritual qualities required for a Christian; a
reiteration and reinterpretation of Moses' laws (especially the
Ten Commandments); the need to avoid showiness, materialism
and judgmentalism; the Lord's Prayer; a warning against false
prophets; and the need to base one's entire life on God. It
contains such important imagery as the Light of the World and
Christ as the fulfilment of the Jewish prophecies, turning the
other cheek, not hiding one's light under a bushel and of God as
a rock on which everything has its foundations.

Our Father which art in Heaven,
Hallowed be thy name.
Thy kingdom come, Thy will be
done on Earth, as it is in Heaven.
Give us this day our daily bread.
And forgive us our debts, as we
forgive our debtors.
And lead us not into temptation,
but deliver us from evil: For thine
is the kingdom, and the power,
and the glory, for ever. Amen.

"THE ACT OF SUPREMACY"
English Parliament

In 1533, Archbishop Thomas Cranmer declared Henry VIII's marriage to his first wife – Catherine of Aragon – null and void, and his second – to Anne Boleyn – legal and valid. Parliament passed various laws limiting the power of the Church and making it subservient to the king. Pope Clement VII, who had refused to annul Henry's first marriage, began excommunication proceedings against both Henry and Cranmer. In response, under Henry's direction, Parliament enacted the Act of Supremacy, which gave the king control over the Church in England, and the Treason Act – which made it treason not to acknowledge the former Act. However, this was not an introduction of Protestantism.

Albeit the King's Majesty justly and rightfully is and ought to be the supreme head of the Church of England, and so is recognized by the clergy of this realm in their convocations, yet nevertheless, for corroboration and confirmation thereof, and for increase of virtue in Christ's religion within this realm of England, and to repress and extirpate all errors, heresies, and other enormities and abuses heretofore used in the same, be it enacted, by authority of this present Parliament, that the king, our sovereign lord, his heirs and successors, kings of this realm, shall be taken, accepted, and reputed the only supreme head on Earth of the Church of England, called Anglicans Ecclesia; and shall have and enjoy, annexed and united to the imperial crown of this realm, as well the title and style thereof, as all honours, dignities, pre-eminences, jurisdictions, privileges, authorities, immunities, profits, and commodities to the said dignity of the supreme head of the same Church belonging and appertaining; and that our said sovereign lord, his heirs and successors, kings of this realm, shall have full power and authority from time to time to visit, repress, redress, record, order, correct, restrain, and amend all such errors, heresies, abuses, offences, contempts and enormities, whatsoever they be, which by any manner of spiritual authority or jurisdiction ought or may lawfully be reformed, repressed, ordered, redressed, corrected, restrained, or amended, most to the pleasure of Almighty God, the increase of virtue in Christ's religion, and for the conservation of the peace, unity, and tranquility of this realm; any usage, foreign land, foreign authority, prescription, or any other thing or things to the contrary hereof notwithstanding.

"95 THESES"
Martin Luther

In the early sixteenth century, there was an increasing divide within the Catholic church about the abuse, particularly the sale, of indulgences – remission of time spent in purgatory after death for sins already forgiven – allowing people to buy their way out of sins rather than confession and contrition. The papal commissioner for indulgences was sent to Germany to sell them in order to fund the rebuilding of St Peter's Basilica in Rome. Luther's 95 Theses are a response to this mission, intended as the basis for a debate at the University of Wittenberg. A copy is said to have been stuck to the door of the Castle Church in Wittenberg – a church with thousands of relics that the pious could pay to see and so gain an indulgence. It was intended that the whole life of believers should be penitence.

1. Our Lord and Master Jesus Christ, in saying 'Repent ye,' etc.,
2. This word cannot be understood of sacramental penance, that is, of the confession and satisfaction which are performed under the ministry of priests.
3. It does not, however, refer solely to inward penitence; nay such inward penitence is naught, unless it outwardly produces various mortifications of the flesh.
4. The Penalty thus continues as long as the hatred of self – that is, true inward penitence – continues: namely, till our entrance into the kingdom of Heaven.
5. The Pope has neither the will nor the power to remit any penalties, except those which he has imposed by his own authority, or by that of the canons.
6. The Pope has no power to remit any guilt, except by declaring and warranting it to have been remitted by God; or at most by remitting cases reserved for himself; in which cases, if his power were despised, guilt would certainly remain.

7. God never remits any man's guilt, without at the same time subjecting him, humbled in all things, to the authority of his representative the priest . . .

20. Therefore the Pope, when he speaks of the plenary remission of all penalties, does not mean simply of all, but only of those imposed by himself.

21. Thus those preachers of indulgences are in error who say that, by the indulgences of the Pope, a man is loosed and saved from all punishment.

22. For in fact he remits to souls in purgatory no penalty which they would have had to pay in this life according to the canons . . .

31. Rare as is a true penitent, so rare is one who truly buys indulgences – that is to say, most rare.

32. Those who believe that, through letters of pardon, they are made sure of their own salvation, will be eternally damned along with their teachers.

33. We must especially beware of those who say that these pardons from the Pope are that inestimable gift of God by which man is reconciled to God . . .

36. Every Christian who feels true compunction has of right plenary remission of pain and guilt, even without letters of pardon.

37. Every true Christian, whether living or dead, has a share in all the benefits of Christ and of the Church given him by God, even without letters of pardon . . .

40. True contrition seeks and loves punishment; while the ampleness of pardons relaxes it, and causes men to hate it, or at least gives occasion for them to do so.

41. Apostolical pardons ought to be proclaimed with caution, lest the people should falsely suppose that they are placed before other good works of charity . . .

44. Because, by a work of charity, charity increases and the man becomes better; while, by means of pardons, he does not become better, but only freer from punishment.

45. Christians should be taught that he who sees any one in need, and passing him by, gives money for pardons, is not purchasing for himself the indulgences of the Pope, but the anger of God . . .

48. Christians should be taught that the Pope, in granting pardons, has both more need and more desire that devout prayer should be

made for him, than that money should be readily paid . . .

52. Vain is the hope of salvation through letters of pardon, even if a commissary – nay, the Pope himself – were to pledge his own soul for them . . .

58. Nor are they the merits of Christ and of the saints, for these, independently of the Pope, are always working grace to the inner man, and the cross, death, and hell to the outer man . . .

67. Those indulgences, which the preachers loudly proclaim to be the greatest graces, are seen to be truly such as regards the promotion of gain . . .

76. We affirm, on the contrary, that Papal pardons cannot take away even the least of venal sins, as regards its guilt . . .

84. Again: what is this new kindness of God and the Pope, in that, for money's sake, they permit an impious man and an enemy of God to redeem a pious soul which loves God, and yet do not redeem that same pious and beloved soul, out of free charity, on account of its own need? . . .

88. Again: what greater good would the Church receive if the Pope, instead of once, as he does now, were to bestow these remissions and participations a hundred times a day on any one of the faithful? . . .

94. Christians should be exhorted to strive to follow Christ their Head through pains, deaths, and hells.

95. And thus trust to enter Heaven through many tribulations, rather than in the security of peace.

"THE FAMILY THEATER
RADIO SERIES"
Al Scalpone

In 1947, a Roman Catholic priest from South Bend, Indiana, Patrick Peyton, founder of the Family Rosary Crusade, began a radio series called *Family Theater* in order to use first the radio, and then later television, to promote prayer, moral values and family stability. The programmes featured Hollywood stars such as James Stewart, Don Ameche, William Shatner, Loretta Young, Shirley Temple, Placido Domingo, Frank Sinatra and Grace Kelly (her last three television appearances were on the show). A young advertising executive, Al Scalpone, wrote the famous slogan for the radio show in 1947, and it appeared on billboards all over the USA.

The family that prays together stays together.

"THE FIRST BLAST OF THE TRUMPET AGAINST THE MONSTROUS REGIMENT OF WOMEN"
John Knox

In 1558, the Protestant reformer launched a series of verbal and written attacks against the – to him – almost heretical idea that a woman could rule over a country. At this time, both England and Scotland were ruled by Catholic women: the former by Mary I and the latter by Mary of Guise as regent for her daughter, Mary, Queen of Scots. In pamphlet form, 'The First Blast of the Trumpet Against the Monstrous Regiment of Women' was published in Geneva in 1558.

Wonder it is, that amongst so many pregnant wits as the Isle of Great Britain hath produced, so many godly and zealous preachers as England did sometime nourish, and amongst so many learned and men of grave judgment, as this day by Jezebel are exiled, none is found so stout of courage, so faithful to God, nor loving to their native country, that they dare admonish the inhabitants of that Isle how abominable before God, is the Empire or Rule of a wicked woman, yea of a traitor and bastard . . . we hear the blood of our brethren, the members of Christ Jesus most cruelly to be shed, and the monstrous empire of a cruel woman (the secret counsel of God excepted) we know to be the only occasion of all these miseries: and yet with silence we pass the time as though the matter did nothing appertain to us . . .

. . . I am assured that God hath revealed to some in this our age, that it is more than a monster in nature, that a woman shall reign and have empire above man. And yet with us all, there is such silence, as if God therewith were nothing offended . . . If any think that the empire of women, is not of such importance, that for the suppressing of the same, any man is bound to hazard his life, I answer, that to suppress it, is in the hand of God alone. But to utter the impiety and abomination of the same, I say, it is the duty of every true messager of God, to whom the truth is revealed in that behalf . . . I say, that of necessity it is, that, this monstiferous empire of women, (which amongst all enormities, that this day do abound upon the face of the whole Earth, is most detestable and damnable) be openly revealed and plainly declared to the world, to the end that some may repent and be saved . . .

. . . For who can deny but it is repugnant to nature, that the blind shall be appointed to lead and conduct such as do see? That the weak, the sick and impotent persons shall nourish and keep the whole and strong? And finally, that the foolish, mad and phrenetic shall govern the discrete . . . And such be all women, compared unto man in bearing of authority. For their sight in civil regiment is but blindness; their strength, weakness; their counsel, foolishnes; and judgment, frenzy, if it be rightly considered.

SCIENCE

"THE THEORY ON EVOLUTION THROUGH NATURAL SELECTION"
Charles Darwin

Darwin had delayed publishing his theory on evolution through
natural selection for many years, and it was only when Alfred
Russell Wallace sent him his paper with similar ideas that he
decided to publish. He sent extracts from his manuscript (which
botanist Joseph Hooker had read in 1844), along with Wallace's
paper to the geologist Charles Lyell, who, with Hooker, decided
that the best course would be to publish both together, along
with a letter of Darwin's from 1847, confirming that he had
precedence. The two papers were read on 1 July, 1858 at the
Linnean Society in London. There was not much reaction at the
time: that came in the following year with the publication of
Darwin's *On the Origin of Species by Means of Natural Selection,
or the Preservation of Favoured Races in the Struggle for Life.*

De Candolle, in an eloquent passage, has declared that all nature is
at ear, one organism with another, or with external nature. Seeing
the contented face of nature, this may at first well be doubted; but
reflection will inevitably prove it to be true. The war, however,
is not constant, but recurrent in a slight degree at short periods,
and more severely at occasional more distant periods; and hence

its effects are easily overlooked. It is the doctrine of Malthus applied in most cases with tenfold force. As in every climate there are seasons, for each of its inhabitants, of greater and less abundance, so all annually breed; and the moral restraint which in some small degree checks the increase of mankind is entirely lost. Even slow-breeding mankind has doubled in 25 years; and if he could increase his food with greater ease, he would double in less time. But for animals without artificial means, the amount of food for each species must, on an average, be constant, whereas the increase of all organisms tends to be geometrical, and in a vast majority of cases at an enormous ratio. Suppose in a certain spot there are eight pairs of birds, and that only four pairs of them annually (including double hatches) rear only four young, and that these go on rearing their young at the same rate, then at the end of seven years (a short life, excluding violent deaths, for any bird) there will be 2048 birds, instead of the original sixteen. As this increase is quite impossible, we must conclude either that birds do not rear nearly half their young, or that the average life of a bird is, from accident, not nearly seven years. Both checks probably concur. The same kind of calculation applied to all plants and animals affords results more or less striking, but in very few instances more striking than in man.

Many practical illustrations of this rapid tendency to increase are on record, among which, during peculiar seasons, are the extraordinary numbers of certain animals; for instance, during the years 1826 to 1828, in La Plata, when from drought some millions of cattle perished, the whole country actually swarmed with mice. Now I think it cannot be doubted that during the breeding season all the mice (with the exception of a few males or females in excess) ordinarily pair, and therefore that this astounding increase during three years must be attributed to a greater number than usual surviving the first year, and then breeding, and so on till the third year, when their numbers were brought down to their usual limits on the return of wet weather. Where man has introduced plants and animals into a new and favourable country, there are many accounts in how surprisingly few years the whole country has become stocked with them. This increase would necessarily stop as soon as the country was fully stocked; and yet we have every reason to believe, from what is known of wild animals, that all would pair in the spring. In the majority of cases it is most difficult to imagine where the checks fall – though generally, no doubt, on the seeds, eggs, and young; but when we remember how impossible, even in mankind (so much better known than any other animal), it is to infer from repeated casual observations what the average duration of life is, or to discover the different percentage of deaths to births in different countries, we ought to feel no surprise at our being unable to discover where the check falls in any animal or plant. It should always be remembered, that in most cases the checks are recurrent yearly in a small, regular degree, and in an extreme degree during unusually cold, hot, dry, or wet years, according to the constitution of the being in question. Lighten any check in the least degree, and the geometrical powers of increase in every organism will almost instantly increase the average number of the favoured species. Nature may be compared to a surface on which rest ten thousand sharp wedges touching each other and driven inwards by incessant blows. Fully to realize these views much reflection is requisite. Malthus on man should be studied; and all such cases as those of the mice in La Plata, of the cattle and horses when first turned out in South America, of the birds by our calculation, &c., should be well considered. Reflect on the enormous multiplying power inherent and annually in action in all animals; reflect on the countless seeds scattered by a hundred ingenious contrivances, year after year, over the whole face of the land; and yet we have every reason to suppose that the average percentage of each of the inhabitants of a country usually remains constant. Finally, let it be borne in mind that this average number of individuals (the external conditions remaining the same) in each country is kept up by recurrent struggles against other species or against external nature (as on the borders of the Arctic regions, where the cold checks life), and that ordinarily each individual of every species holds its place, either by its own struggle and capacity of acquiring nourishment in some period of its life, from the egg upwards; or by the struggle of its parents (in short-lived organisms, when the main check occurs at longer intervals) with other individuals of the same or different species.

But let the external conditions of a country alter. If in a small degree, the relative proportions of the inhabitants will in most cases simply be slightly changed; but let the number of inhabitants be small, as on an island, and free access to it from other countries be circumscribed, and let the change of conditions continue progressing (forming new stations), in such a case the original inhabitants must cease to be as perfectly adapted to the changed conditions as they were originally. It has been shown in a former part of this work, that such changes of external conditions would, from their acting on the reproductive system, probably cause the organization of those beings which were most affected to become, as under domestication, plastic. Now, can it be doubted, from the struggle each individual has to obtain subsistence, that any minute variation in structure, habits, or instincts, adapting that individual better to the new conditions, would tell upon its vigour and health? In the struggle it would have a better chance of surviving; and those of its offspring which inherited the variation, be it ever so slight, would also have a better chance. Yearly more are bred than can survive; the smallest grain in the balance, in the long run, must tell on which death shall fall, and which shall survive. Let this work of selection on the one hand, and death on the other, go on for a thousand generations, who will pretend to affirm that it would produce no effect, when we remember what, in a few years, Bakewell effected in cattle, and Western in sheep, by this identical principle of selection?

To give an imaginary example from changes in progress on an island: – let the organization of a canine animal which preyed chiefly on rabbits, but sometimes on hares, become slightly plastic; let these same changes cause the number of rabbits very slowly to decrease, and the number of hares to increase; the effect of this would be that the fox or dog would be driven to try to catch more hares: his organization, however, being slightly plastic, those individuals with the lightest forms, longest limbs, and best eyesight, let the difference be ever so small, would be slightly favoured, and would tend to live longer, and to survive during that time of the year when food was scarcest; they would also rear more young, which would tend to inherit these slight peculiarities. The less fleet ones would be rigidly destroyed. I can see no more reason to doubt that these causes in a thousand generations would produce a marked effect, and adapt the form of the fox or dog to the catching of hares instead of rabbits, than that greyhounds can be improved by selection and careful breeding. So would it be with plants under similar circumstances. If the number of individuals of a species with plumed seeds could be increased by greater powers of dissemination within its own area (that is, if the check to increase fell chiefly on the seeds), those seeds which were provided with ever so little more down, would in the long run be most disseminated; hence a greater number of seeds thus formed would germinate, and would tend to produce plants inheriting the slightly better-adapted down.

Besides this natural means of selection, by which those individuals are preserved, whether in their egg, or larval, or mature state, which are best adapted to the place they fill in nature, there is a second agency at work in most unisexual animals, tending to produce the same effect, namely, the struggle of the males for the females. These struggles are generally decided by the law of battle, but in the case of birds, apparently, by the charms of their song, by their beauty or their power of courtship, as in the dancing rock-thrush of Guiana. The most vigorous and healthy males, implying perfect adaptation, must generally gain the victory in their contests. This kind of selection, however, is less rigorous than the other; it does not require the death of the less successful, but gives to them fewer descendants. The struggle falls, moreover, at a time of year when food is generally abundant, and perhaps the effect chiefly produced would be the modification of the secondary sexual characters, which are not related to the power of obtaining food, or to defence from enemies, but to fighting with or rivalling other males. The result of this struggle amongst the males may be compared in some respects to that produced by those agriculturists who pay less attention to the careful selection of all their young animals, and more to the occasional use of a choice mate.

"THE MOON IS MADE OF EARTH"
Anaxagoras

Anaxagoras was an early Greek philosopher, many of whose ideas were not accepted by the majority of his fellow philosophers, even though they have subsequently been proved to be right. His theory that everything is made up of minute particles eventually led to the atomic theory. He correctly described how solar and lunar eclipses occur (although he may not have been the first to do so) and asserted that stars were masses of stone. These views were seen as dangerous because they questioned the current religious beliefs about the cosmos – this in an era when the majority believed that natural phenomena were under the control of gods who were liable to react to heresy with earthquakes or some other misfortune – and he was imprisoned until Athens' leader, Pericles, got him released.

We do not feel the heat of the stars because they are so far from the Earth . . . The Moon has no light of its own but derives it from the Sun . . . The Moon is made of Earth and has plains and ravines on it.

"PREDICTABILITY: DOES THE FLAP OF A BUTTERFLY'S WINGS IN BRAZIL SET OFF A TORNADO IN TEXAS?"
Edward Lorenz

Meteorologist and mathematician Edward Lorenz had noticed in
the 1960s that even very small changes in data input into
computer models of weather made significant differences
to forecasts. On 29 December, 1972 he gave a lecture to the
American Association for the Advancement of Science's
139th meeting, with the title 'Predictability; Does the Flap of
a Butterfly's wings in Brazil Set Off a Tornado in Texas?' His
conclusion was that it was impossible to say. However, he did
point out that small-scale differences in the atmosphere that
were not at that time observable by the instruments available to
weather forecasters could generate larger-scale discrepancies
between a forecast and the real weather.

. . . If a single flap of a butterfly's wings can be instrumental in
generating a tornado, so also in all the previous and subsequent
flaps of its wings, as can the flaps of the wings of millions of other
butterflies, not to mention the activities of innumerable more
powerful creatures, including our own species . . .
    . . . The question which really interests us is whether they can do
even this – whether, for example, two particular weather situations
differing by as little as the immediate influence of a single butterfly
will generally after sufficient time evolve into two situations
differing by as much as the presence of a tornado.

"GIVE ME A LEVER . . . AND I'LL MOVE THE WORLD"
Archimedes

Archimedes was probably the ancient world's greatest engineer, astronomer, physicist and mathematician. He invented many geometrical formulae, came up with the principles of weighing objects through the displacement of water – which led to his famous 'Eureka!' moment – and calculated the value of Pi extremely accurately. He also demonstrated the principle of the lever – the relationship between the distance and weight of an object from the lever's fulcrum and those of the counterweight at the other end of the lever – which led to the quotation below. Although he preferred pure mathematics, he put his knowledge to practical use, creating siege engines designed to protect the city, although they did not prevent the Romans taking Syracuse in 212 BCE, when he was killed by a soldier for refusing to accompany him because he was finishing a calculation.

Give me a lever, a fulcrum and a firm place to stand and I will move the world.

"THE HIPPOCRATIC OATH"
Hippocrates

Hippocrates is widely known as the father of Western medicine. He rejected the idea that illness was caused by divine or magical intervention in favour of the theory that the body contained four fluids (humours) – blood, black bile, yellow bile and phlegm – that maintained health. Illness occurred when these were not in balance. Although this part of his theory is no longer believed, his teachings on lung disease are still valid and haemorrhoids are still treated in more or less the same way as he advocated. The Declaration of Geneva is the World Medical Association's equivalent of the Hippocratic Oath and there are various modern forms of the Oath in different countries, reflecting changes in medical practice and culture.

I swear by Apollo, Asclepius, Hygieia, and Panacea, and I take to witness all the gods, all the goddesses, to keep according to my ability and my judgment, the following Oath.

To consider dear to me, as my parents, him who taught me this art; to live in common with him and, if necessary, to share my goods with him; To look upon his children as my own brothers, to teach them this art.

I will prescribe regimens for the good of my patients according to my ability and my judgment and never do harm to anyone.

I will not give a lethal drug to anyone if I am asked, nor will I advise such a plan; and similarly I will not give a woman a pessary to cause an abortion.

But I will preserve the purity of my life and my arts.

I will not cut for stone, even for patients in whom the disease is manifest; I will leave this operation to be performed by practitioners, specialists in this art.

In every house where I come I will enter only for the good of my patients, keeping myself far from all intentional ill-doing and all seduction and especially from the pleasures of love with women or with men, be they free or slaves.

All that may come to my knowledge in the exercise of my profession or in daily commerce with men, which ought not to be spread abroad, I will keep secret and will never reveal.

If I keep this oath faithfully, may I enjoy my life and practice my art, respected by all men and in all times; but if I swerve from it or violate it, may the reverse be my lot.

"THE UNIVERSAL LAW OF GRAVITATION"
Isaac Newton

For two years from 1666 Isaac Newton was forced to live at his mother's home in the village of Woolsthorpe because Cambridge University was closed due to a plague epidemic. Whether or not the apple story is true, it was during this period that he formulated his laws of gravitation, realizing that gravity is universal and that the force it exerts diminishes over distance and is symmetrical between two objects. The equation for the Universal Law of Gravitation can be written as below, which means that the force is proportional to the masses of the two objects multiplied together but inversely proportional to their distance apart, i.e., two objects placed two feet apart will exert only a quarter of the gravitational force that they would if placed one foot apart.

$F = GM_1M_2/d_2$

F = the attractive force between two bodies of masses M_1 and M_2, separated by the distance and G is the Universal Gravitational Constant . . . if it universally appears, by experiments and astronomical observations, that all bodies about the Earth, gravitate toward the Earth; and that in proportion to the quantity of matter which they severally contain; that the Moon likewise, according to the quantity of its matter, gravitates toward the Earth; that on the other hand our sea gravitates toward the Moon; and all the planets mutually one toward another; and the comets in like manner towards the Sun; we must, in consequence of this rule, universally allow, that all bodies whatsoever are endowed with a principle of mutual gravitation. For the argument from the appearances concludes with more force for the universal gravitation of all bodies, than for their impenetrability, of which among those in the celestial regions, we have no experiments, nor any manner of observation. Not that I affirm gravity to be essential to all bodies. By their inherent force I mean nothing but their force of inertia. This is immutable. Their gravity is diminished as they recede from the Earth.

(From the 1729 translation of Principia by A. Motte)

"AN INCONVENIENT TRUTH"
Al Gore

Al Gore, US Vice-President for eight years from 1992 to 2000, and former Presidential candidate, has long been a campaigner on environmental issues, especially since 2001 in the face of the US government's hostility to the concept of anthropogenic global warming and such measures as the Kyoto Protocol. He had given his lecture about climate change more than 1,000 times before it was adapted to the film *An Inconvenient Truth*, allowing his message to reach a much wider audience. It is one of the highest-grossing films of all time and won the 2007 Academy Award for best documentary feature. The text below is from the opening monologue, reminding viewers just what might be lost if the scientists' worst predictions are right.

You look at that river gently flowing by. You notice the leaves rustling with the wind. You hear the birds; you hear the tree frogs. In the distance you hear a cow. You feel the grass. The mud gives a little bit on the river bank. It's quiet; it's peaceful. And all of a sudden, it's a gear shift inside you. And it's like taking a deep breath and going . . . 'Oh yeah, I forgot about this.'

"WATCHING HIROSHIMA"
J. Robert Oppenheimer

Just three weeks before a nuclear bomb was dropped on the Japanese city of Hiroshima, the technology was tested in practice for the first time. It was an implosion-design plutonium bomb, like that which would be dropped on Nagasaki on 9 August. The director of The Manhattan Project was J. Robert Oppenheimer who murmured this line from the Hindu Bhagavad Gita as he watched the explosion; although in some versions of the story he just thought it to himself. Because of his communist connections and political activities in the 1930s he was always under suspicion and had to appear in front of the House Un-American Activities Committee in 1953, after which he was stripped of his security clearance and lost his job.

Now I am become Death, the destroyer of worlds.

"A CAUSE FOR UNPREDICTABILITY"
Albert Einstein

•

One of the most brilliant scientists ever, Einstein did not agree
with one of the basic tenets of quantum physics: that at the
microphysical level the workings of classical Newtonian physics
do not apply and it is impossible to determine, for example,
in an atom where any one of its electrons might be, only the
probability of where it might be. He argued that there must be a
deterministic cause for this unpredictability: it was simply that
it had not yet been found, whereas other physicists like Niels
Bohr and Werner Heisenberg believed that the behaviour of the
fundamental constituents of matter is entirely random. No cause
has yet been found.

God does not play dice with the Universe.

"FIRST WORDS SPOKEN ON THE TELEPHONE"
Alexander Graham Bell

On 10th March, 1876, the inventor Alexander Graham Bell spoke to his assistant Thomas Watson through his recently patented device. His voice vibrated a diaphragm, which moved a needle and caused a variation in an attached electrical circuit. This was transmitted along a wire to a similar receiver in the next room, and his assistant heard the words clearly. He called this invention an 'acoustic telegraph'. The device caught on quickly wherever he demonstrated it and by 1886 more than 150,000 people in the USA had telephones, incorporating such improvements as Thomas Edison's carbon microphone which picked up sounds much better than the original diaphragm.

Mr Watson, come here: I want you.

PATRIOTISM

"I ADVANCE WITH OBEDIENCE TO THE WORK . . ."
Thomas Jefferson

After the very closely fought Presidential election of 1800, Thomas Jefferson was declared the winner only in late February 1801. In his inaugural address, 25 years after he had drafted the Declaration of Independence, he set out his vision for the future of America with low taxes, as little interference from the US Government in people's daily lives as possible, equal justice for all and peaceful relations with other nations. His gratitude that a wide ocean separated the USA from the squabbling countries of Europe formed a cornerstone of his foreign policy: the non-interference that lasted for generations and presaged the Monroe Doctrine.

Called upon to undertake the duties of the first executive office of our country, I avail myself of the presence of that portion of my fellow citizens which is here assembled to express my grateful thanks for the favour with which they have been pleased to look toward me, to declare a sincere consciousness that the task is above my talents, and that I approach it with those anxious and awful presentiments which the greatness of the charge and the weakness of my powers so justly inspire. A rising nation, spread over a wide and fruitful land, traversing all the seas with the rich productions of their industry, engaged in commerce with nations who feel power and forget right, advancing rapidly to destinies beyond the reach of mortal eye – when I contemplate these transcendent objects, and see the honour, the happiness, and the hopes of this beloved country committed to the issue, and the auspices of this day, I shrink from the contemplation, and humble myself before the magnitude of the undertaking. Utterly, indeed, should I despair did not the presence of many whom I here see remind me that in the other high authorities provided by our Constitution I shall find resources of wisdom, of virtue, and of zeal on which to rely under all difficulties . . .

Let us, then, with courage and confidence pursue our own Federal and Republican principles, our attachment to union and representative government. Kindly separated by nature and a wide ocean from the exterminating havoc of one quarter of the globe; too high-minded to endure the degradations of the others; possessing a chosen country, with room enough for our descendants to the thousandth and thousandth generation; entertaining a due sense of our equal right to the use of our own faculties, to the acquisitions of our own industry, to honour and confidence from our fellow-citizens, resulting not from birth, but from our actions and their sense of them; enlightened by a benign religion, professed, indeed, and practiced in various forms, yet all of them inculcating honesty, truth, temperance, gratitude, and the love of man; acknowledging and adoring an overruling Providence, which by all its dispensations proves that it delights in the happiness of man here and his greater happiness hereafter – with all these blessings, what more is necessary to make us a happy and a prosperous people? Still one thing more, fellow-citizens – a wise and frugal Government, which shall restrain men from injuring one another, shall leave them otherwise free to regulate their own pursuits of industry and improvement, and shall not take from the mouth of labour the bread it has earned . . .

About to enter, fellow-citizens, on the exercise of duties which comprehend everything dear and valuable to you, it is proper you should understand what I deem the essential principles of our Government, and consequently those which ought to shape its Administration. I will compress them within the narrowest compass they will bear, stating the general principle, but not all its limitations. Equal and exact justice to all men, of whatever state or persuasion, religious or political; peace, commerce, and honest friendship with all nations, entangling alliances with none; the support of the State governments in all their rights, as the most competent administrations for our domestic concerns and the surest bulwarks against antirepublican tendencies; the preservation of the General Government in its whole constitutional vigour, as the sheet anchor of our peace at home and safety abroad; a jealous care of the right of election by the people – a mild and safe corrective of abuses which are lopped by the sword of revolution where peaceable remedies are unprovided; absolute acquiescence in the decisions of the majority, the vital principle of republics, from which is no appeal but to force, the vital principle and immediate parent of despotism; a well disciplined militia, our best reliance in peace and for the first moments of war, till regulars may relieve them; the supremacy of the civil over the military authority; economy in the public expense, that labour may be lightly burthened; the honest payment of our debts and sacred preservation of the public faith; encouragement of agriculture, and of commerce as its handmaid; the diffusion of information and arraignment of all abuses at the bar of the public reason; freedom of religion; freedom of the press, and freedom of person under the protection of the habeas corpus, and trial by juries impartially selected. These principles form the bright constellation which has gone before us and guided our steps through an age of revolution and reformation. The wisdom of our sages and blood of our heroes have been devoted to their attainment. They should be the creed of our political faith, the text of civic instruction, the touchstone by which to try the services of those we trust; and should we wander from them in moments of error or of alarm, let us hasten to retrace our steps and to regain the road which alone leads to peace, liberty, and safety . . .

Relying, then, on the patronage of your good will, I advance with obedience to the work, ready to retire from it whenever you become sensible how much better choice it is in your power to make. And may that Infinite Power which rules the destinies of the universe lead our councils to what is best, and give them a favourable issue for your peace and prosperity.

"THE LAST WORDS OF CAPTAIN HALE"
Nathan Hale

A year into the American Revolutionary War, and just days after the signing of the Declaration of Independence, the British Navy moved on New York City. After the ensuing Battle of Long Island on 27 August, George Washington first moved his troops to Brooklyn Heights, and then made a strategic withdrawal to Manhattan Island, where further battles were fought. On 21 September Captain Hale of the Continental Army was captured during a reconnaissance mission. He was taken to the British Commander, General Howe, and the following morning hanged as a spy. He is reported to have given a long, eloquent speech, of which these were the last words.

I only regret, that I have but one life to lose for my country.

"BEFORE THE BATTLE OF TRAFALGAR"
Horatio Nelson

During the interminable wars with France and a variety of coalitions between other European nations (1792–1815) battles were fought on land and at sea from Moscow to the Atlantic and from the English Channel to Egypt. In 1805 the British navy was blockading the Franco-Spanish fleet in the port of Cadiz. When the enemy ships slipped out of the harbour, the British pursued them. Just before the Battle of Trafalgar commenced, Admiral Nelson had the following flag signal raised on HMS *Victory*. Nelson's tactics of attacking from the side in two divisions were highly successful: he lost no ships in the melée while the Franco-Spanish fleet lost 18.

England expects that every man will do his duty.

"TAKE ROME OR PERISH"
Giuseppe Garibaldi

Despite his failure to keep hold of Rome in 1849, Italian patriot Giuseppe Garibaldi decided to make another attempt in 1862. The Papal States – modern-day Lazio, Umbria, Marche and the Romagna area of Emilia-Romagna – were under the direct control of the Popes in Rome and formed a division between the other two parts of the Italian peninsula. As he set out from Catania, Garibaldi swore that he would either take Rome or perish beneath its walls. He had convinced himself that he had the clandestine support of the government, but was mistaken; he was met by an army and rather than making a fight of it he forbade his soldiers to fire on fellow soldiers of the Kingdom of Italy and surrendered.

Roma o Morte! (Rome or Death!)

"GLORY, GLORY, HALLELUJAH!"
Julia Ward Howe

Poet and abolitionist Julia Ward Howe heard the Unionist marching song *John Brown's Body* at a review of troops on 18 November, 1861 and later said that she woke up the next morning with the words of the following battle hymn running through her head. They were published in *The Atlantic Monthly* magazine the following February. The song is still widely referenced in literature (Steinbeck's *The Grapes of Wrath*, for example), films and other popular culture. It has been played at the funerals of several presidents, as well as that of Sir Winston Churchill.

Mine eyes have seen the glory of the coming of the Lord:
He is trampling out the vintage where the grapes of wrath are stored;
He hath loosed the fateful lightning of His terrible swift sword:
His truth is marching on.
(Chorus)
Glory, glory, hallelujah!
Glory, glory, hallelujah!
Glory, glory, hallelujah!
His truth is marching on.
I have seen Him in the watch-fires of a hundred circling camps,
They have builded Him an altar in the evening dews and damps;
I can read His righteous sentence by the dim and flaring lamps:
His day is marching on.
(Chorus)
Glory, glory, hallelujah!
Glory, glory, hallelujah!
Glory, glory, hallelujah!
His day is marching on.
I have read a fiery gospel writ in burnished rows of steel:

As ye deal with my contemners, so with you my grace shall deal;
Let the Hero, born of woman, crush the serpent with his heel,
Since God is marching on.
(Chorus)
Glory, glory, hallelujah!
Glory, glory, hallelujah!
Glory, glory, hallelujah!
Since God is marching on.
He has sounded forth the trumpet that shall never call retreat;
He is sifting out the hearts of men before His judgment-seat:
Oh, be swift, my soul, to answer Him! be jubilant, my feet!
Our God is marching on.
(Chorus)
Glory, glory, hallelujah!
Glory, glory, hallelujah!
Glory, glory, hallelujah!
Our God is marching on.
In the beauty of the lilies Christ was born across the sea,
With a glory in His bosom that transfigures you and me:
As He died to make men holy, let us die to make men free,
While God is marching on.
(Chorus)
Glory, glory, hallelujah!
Glory, glory, hallelujah!
Glory, glory, hallelujah!
While God is marching on.
He is coming like the glory of the morning on the wave,
He is Wisdom to the mighty, He is Succour to the brave,
So the world shall be His footstool, and the soul of Time His slave,
Our God is marching on.
(Chorus)
Glory, glory, hallelujah!
Glory, glory, hallelujah!
Glory, glory, hallelujah!
Our God is marching on.

"DECATUR'S TOAST"
Stephen Decatur

Stephen Decatur – a naval hero of the First and Second Barbary Wars and the War of 1812 against the British – is the originator of a famously misquoted sentence. His toast at a dinner in April 1816 – known as Decatur's Toast – is usually rendered as 'My country, right or wrong', implying an unthinking patriotism bordering on redneck jingoism, but his original version is a pledge of loyalty to his country even when he knows it is in the wrong. Decatur was killed in a duel with Commodore James Barron, on whose court-martial he had served and about whose conduct he had made severe remarks. He was so famous a hero that five US Navy ships, 46 communities and several schools and roads were named after him.

Our country! In her intercourse with foreign nations, may she always be in the right; but our country, right or wrong!

PHILOSOPHY

"DISCOURSE ON METHOD"
René Descartes

Descartes is regarded as the founder of modern Western philosophy, and this simple maxim is one of its founding arguments, published in his *Discourse on Method*. The statement – often used in the Latin, *Cogito, ergo sum*, means that he only knew that he existed because he was a thinking being. If someone doubts whether he or she exists, it is proof that he or she does. The senses are not to be trusted, as they can be mistaken. He used the example of a piece of wax that, when heated, becomes different from when it was cold. It was only through thinking, that he knew that the solid and melted wax were the same thing.

Je pense donce je suis. (I think, therefore I am.)

"POLITICAL PHILOSOPHY IN *THE REPUBLIC*"

The Republic, which was written circa 380 BCE is one of Plato's Socratic dialogues – fictionalised accounts of discussions between Greek philosophers. In the section on political philosophy, a discussion between Socrates and Glaucius debates what sort of people are fit to rule. At this time, rule in Athens was divided among a select few and those who got their way tended to be those who used persuasion through clever use of words rather than reason and wisdom: how they said something was more important than what they said. He puts the following idea into Socrates' mouth.

Until philosophers are kings, or the kings and princes of this world have the spirit and power of philosophy, and political greatness and wisdom meet in one, and those commoner natures who pursue either to the exclusion of the other are compelled to stand aside, cities will never have rest from their evils, nor the human race, as I believe, and then only will this our State have a possibility of life and behold the light of day.

"THE NATURE OF ANGELS IN THE *SUMMA THEOLOGICA*"
Thomas Aquinas

Although St Thomas Aquinas did not actually ever ask how
many angels could dance on the end of a needle, he and fellow
Scholastics (who combined theology with classical Greek and
Roman thought) did debate very obscure theological issues,
including the number and nature of angels, whether one's hair
and fingernails would grow after the resurrection and even
whether excrement existed in heaven. His *Summa Theologica*
(1267–1273) contains a summation of this, including the
following passage about whether angels have any corporeal
(that is, material) form or were entirely spiritual. The minute
arguments of the Scholastics were lampooned in later years as
pointless debates about meaningless issues.

Some assert that the angels are composed of matter and form
. . . but one glance is enough to show that there cannot be one
matter of spiritual and of corporeal things. For it is not possible
that a spiritual and a corporeal form should be received into the
same part of matter, otherwise one and the same thing would
be corporeal and spiritual. Hence it would follow that one part
of matter receives the corporeal form, and another receives the
spiritual form. Matter, however, is not divisible into parts except
as regarded under quantity; and without quantity substance is
indivisible, as Aristotle says. Therefore it would follow that the
matter of spiritual things is subject to quantity; which cannot
be. Therefore it is impossible that corporeal and spiritual things
should have the same matter.

It is, further, impossible for an intellectual substance to have
any kind of matter. For the operation belonging to anything is
according to the mode of its substance. Now to understand is
an altogether immaterial operation, as appears from its object,

whence any act receives its species and nature. For a thing is understood according to its degree of immateriality; because forms that exist in matter are individual forms which the intellect cannot apprehend as such. Hence it must be that every individual substance is altogether immaterial.

"THE NECESSITY OF GOD"
Voltaire

Voltaire was one of the leading thinkers of the Enlightenment in France and, because of strict censorship laws, was often under threat from the authorities at a time when the nobility could get troublemakers imprisoned or exiled without trial. This led him to campaign for judicial reform. The church was another of his targets. Many of his contemporaries thought that Voltaire was an atheist, but he described himself as a deist. Although he believed in God, he was highly critical of the activities of the church and organized religion in Europe. And to some extent he regarded the institution of the church as an unnecessary addition to a true belief in a divine being.

If God did not exist, it would be necessary to invent him.

"ALL KNOWLEDGE IS DERIVED FROM EXPERIENCE"
David Hume

David Hume was an early proponent of the school of philosophy known as empiricism. He held that all knowledge is derived from experience, in direct contrast to the ideas of Descartes. His belief that miracles were contrary to the immutable laws of nature and that a witness to one was likely to be genuinely mistaken or lying, led to a charge of heresy from the Church of Scotland. But he was acquitted, possibly on the grounds that as an atheist he was not subject to the church's laws.

When anyone tells me that he saw a dead man restored to life, I immediately consider with myself whether it be more probable that this person should either deceive or be deceived, or that the fact, which he relates should really have happened. I weigh the one miracle against the other; and according to the superiority which I discover, I pronounce my decision and always reject the greater miracle. If the falsehood of his testimony would be more miraculous than the event which he relates; then, and not till then, can he pretend to command my belief or opinion.

"THE GUARD TO THE GUARDS"
Juvenal

The last of the great Roman satirical poets, Juvenal often
denounced the immorality prevalent in Roman society and life.
Very little is known about his life, except that he was probably
born at Aquinum, the modern-day Aquino, southeast of Rome.
There are several biographies of him, but these are all
contradictory. *The Satires* contain diatribes about vice,
hypocrisy, social structure, the city of Rome, women, vanity,
religion, and extravagance, among other things. The line below
is from a passage condemning marriage, saying that it is
pointless setting a guard on a wife who might stray as she will
doubtless tempt. The idea is extended to all those who are in a
position of trust or power, as all people are corruptible.

Sed quis costodiet ipsos Custodes? (But who is to guard the guards
themselves?)

"THE THEORY OF IMMATERIALISM"
George Berkeley

George Berkeley, a tutor and lecturer at Trinity College, Dublin, was the first proponent of the philosophical theory of Immaterialism. In the question below, he addresses the idea that objects exist only when they are perceived by someone or something else and the observer cannot know whether something exists, only that it is perceived. These completely counter-intuitive ideas attracted wide scorn, but in 1713 he published a defence of his argument in which, because God is all-seeing and all-hearing, there is always someone to hear it fall. He summed up the philosophy in his dictum *Esse est percipi* (To be is to be perceived).

If a tree falls in a forest and no-one hears it, does it make a sound?

"MAKING FRIENDS . . ."
Booker T. Washington

At an address given to a white audience on the occasion of the 1895 Atlanta Cotton States and International Exposition, the African-American spokesman and educationalist expressed his ideas about the mutual interdependence of all parts of society, even while different elements of it remained separate. He stressed that for social justice to become a reality, each part of the population should reach out and work together. He believed that government directives about fairness and freedom were pointless without a corresponding bottom-up effort. The sentence about the recognition that agricultural work was as valid as writing poetry became the basis of the idea of useful toil and the dignity of labour.

Not only this, but the opportunity here afforded will awaken among us a new era of industrial progress. Ignorant and inexperienced, it is not strange that in the first years of our new life we began at the top instead of at the bottom; that a seat in Congress or the state legislature was more sought than real estate or industrial skill; that the political convention or stump speaking had more attractions than starting a dairy farm or truck garden.

A ship lost at sea for many days suddenly sighted a friendly vessel. From the mast of the unfortunate vessel was seen a signal, 'Water, water; we die of thirst!' The answer from the friendly vessel at once came back, 'Cast down your bucket where you are.' A second time the signal, 'Water, water; send us water!' ran up from the distressed vessel, and was answered, 'Cast down your bucket where you are.'. And a third and fourth signal for water was answered, 'Cast down your bucket where you are.'. The captain of the distressed vessel, at last heeding the injunction, cast down his bucket, and it came up full of fresh, sparkling water from the mouth of the Amazon River. To those of my race who depend on bettering their condition in a foreign land or who underestimate the importance of cultivating friendly relations with the Southern white man, who is their next-door neighbor, I would say: 'Cast down your bucket where you are.' – cast it down in making friends in every manly way of the people of all races by whom we are surrounded.

Our greatest danger is that in the great leap from slavery to freedom we may overlook the fact that the masses of us are to live by the productions of our hands, and fail to keep in mind that we shall prosper in proportion as we learn to dignify and glorify common labour, and put brains and skill into the common occupations of life; shall prosper in proportion as we learn to draw the line between the superficial and the substantial, the ornamental gewgaws of life and the useful. No race can prosper till it learns that there is as much dignity in tilling a field as in writing a poem. It is at the bottom of life we must begin, and not at the top. Nor should we permit our grievances to overshadow our opportunities.

The wisest among my race understand that the agitation of questions of social equality is the extremist folly, and that progress in the enjoyment of all the privileges that will come to us must be the result of severe and constant struggle rather than of artificial forcing. No race that has anything to contribute to the markets of the world is long in any degree ostracized. It is important and right that all privileges of the law be ours, but it is vastly more important that we be prepared for the exercise of these privileges.

"THE STRUGGLE BETWEEN CLASSES"
Karl Marx

The Marxist definition of proletariat is a class of wage-earners whose only possession of value in a capitalist economy is their labour. In Marxist theory, the dictatorship of the proletariat is a transitional phase between the bourgeois state and a classless, communist one. The word dictatorship signifies democratic rule of one class, not one person, so in the mid-nineteenth century prevailing capitalist culture was the dictatorship of the bourgeoisie. Different schools of Marxism have various ideas about whether or not structures of the bourgeouis state apparatus should be used in the transition or whether it has to be dismantled completely and a new structure imposed.

I do not claim to have discovered either the existence of classes in modern society or the struggle between them. Long before me, bourgeois historians had described the historical development of this struggle between the classes, as had bourgeois economists their economic anatomy. My own contribution was 1. to show that the existence of classes is merely bound up with certain historical phases in the development of production; 2. that the class struggle necessarily leads to the dictatorship of the proletariat; 3. that this dictatorship itself constitutes no more than a transition to the abolition of all classes and to a classless society.

HUMANITY & LIBERTY

"WARNING AFTER THE SIGNING OF THE DECLARATION OF INDEPENDENCE"
Benjamin Franklin

One of the Founding Fathers of America, and one of the signatories of the Declaration of Independence, Benjamin Franklin was a publisher, scientist, inventor, diplomat and writer. From late 1776 until 1785, he was American Commissioner in Paris, and it is in great part due to his efforts that the Franco-American alliance did so much to help America in the later stages of the American Revolutionary War. The signatories to the Declaration of Independence all knew that they were risking the future of the country. The British government had no intention of relinquishing this potentially rich source of income and had declared the entire population rebels – for which the penalty was, indeed, death by hanging.

We must indeed all hang together, or, most assuredly, we shall all hang separately.

"GOD GAVE ME MONEY"
John D. Rockefeller Sr

The epitome of nineteenth-century capitalists, John D.
Rockefeller is to some a sinner and to others a benefactor who
gave away millions of dollars to deserving causes and set up
enormous charitable funds. Perhaps a mixture of both, he was
brought up by his devout mother during the frequent absences
of his wastrel father, which may have been responsible for his
work ethic. He and his business partners hit lucky when they
went into the oil business in the 1860s, but it was his ruthless
business methods – especially his methods of undercutting
his competitors and then buying them out – that led his
company, Standard Oil, to have a virtual monopoly on oil in the
continental US, leading to calls for legal reform. In 1904, Ida
Tarbell, whose father had been forced out of the oil business
by some of Rockefeller's earlier practices, published a scathing
book about the history of Standard Oil, which led to Rockefeller
being vilified and the eventual break-up of the company. It is
during this period that he gave an interview to a journalist,
including what some people saw as the supremely arrogant
comment below.

God gave me my money. I believe the power to make money is
a gift from God . . . to be developed and used to the best of our
ability for the good of mankind. Having been endowed with the
gift I possess, I believe it is my duty to make money and still more
money and to use the money I make for the good of my fellow man
according to the dictates of my conscience.

"REVEALING THE LOFTY ATTITUDE OF SETTLERS IN SOUTH AFRICA"
Cecil Rhodes

Cecil Rhodes left England for South Africa when he was 16 years old. A co-founder of the De Beers Mining Company, farmer and politician, he was instrumental in policies in Cape Colony that resulted in the appalling treatment of black people in southern Africa. In this speech to the Cape Colony House of Assembly during a debate on whether they should be given the vote, he revealed the attitude of many white settlers. He was also instrumental in passing the Glen Grey Act, which legalized the forcible removal of black farmers from their land. As Prime Minister of Cape Colony, he pushed through policies that were of benefit to his own commercial interests, including launching a raid into the Boer Transvaal in 1896, a catastrophic failure that would result in his resignation, his brother being charged with treason and the outbreak of the Second Boer War.

Does this House think that it is right that men in a state of pure barbarism should have the franchise and the vote? . . . Treat the natives as a subject people . . . the native is to be treated as a child and denied the franchise . . . We must adopt a system of despotism such as works so well in India, in our relations with the barbarians of South Africa.

"THE NATIONAL ORGANIZATION FOR WOMEN IS FOUNDED"
The National Organization for Women

**In June 1966, the National Organization for Women was
founded in Washington DC. Later in the year, the first organizing
conference was attended by about 30 of the 300 members.
It came about partly because of discontent at the Equal
Employment Opportunities Commission not enforcing equal-
rights legislation but also because of a persistent lack of rights
for women. In the 1970s the organization supported the Equal
Rights Amendment to the US Constitution.**

We, men and women who hereby constitute ourselves as the
National Organization for Women, believe that the time has come
for a new movement toward true equality for all women in America,
and toward a fully equal partnership of the sexes, as part of the
world-wide revolution of human rights now taking place within and
beyond our national borders.

WE BELIEVE that this nation has a capacity at least as great as
other nations, to innovate new social institutions which will enable
women to enjoy the true equality of opportunity and responsibility
in society, without conflict with their responsibilities as mothers
and homemakers. In such innovations, America does not lead
the Western world, but lags by decades behind many European
countries. We do not accept the traditional assumption that a
woman has to choose between marriage and motherhood, on the
one hand, and serious participation in industry or the professions on
the other. This, in itself, is a deterrent to the aspirations of women,
to their acceptance into management or professional training
courses, and to the very possibility of equality of opportunity
or real choice, for all but a few women. Above all, we reject the
assumption that these problems are the unique responsibility of
each individual woman, rather than a basic social dilemma which

society must solve. True equality of opportunity and freedom of choice for women requires such practical and possible innovations as a nationwide network of child-care centers, which will make it unnecessary for women to retire completely from society until their children are grown, and national programs to provide retraining for women who have chosen to care for their children full-time.

WE BELIEVE that it is as essential for every girl to be educated to her full potential of human ability as it is for every boy – with the knowledge that such education is the key to effective participation in today's economy and that, for a girl as for a boy, education can only be serious where there is expectation that it will be used in society . . . Moreover, we consider the decline in the proportion of women receiving higher and professional education to be evidence of discrimination. This discrimination may take the form of quotas against the admission of women to colleges and professional schools; lack of encouragement by parents, counselors and educators; denial of loans or fellowships; or the traditional or arbitrary procedures in graduate and professional training geared in terms of men, which inadvertently discriminate against women. We believe that the same serious attention must be given to high school dropouts who are girls as to boys . . .

WE BELIEVE that women must now exercise their political rights and responsibilities as American citizens. They must refuse to be segregated on the basis of sex into separate-and-not-equal ladies' auxiliaries in the political parties, and they must demand representation according to their numbers in the regularly constituted party committees – at local, state, and national levels – and in the informal power structure, participating fully in the selection of candidates and political decision-making, and running for office themselves . . .

WE BELIEVE THAT women will do most to create a new image of women by acting now, and by speaking out in behalf of their own equality, freedom, and human dignity – not in pleas for special privilege, nor in enmity toward men, who are also victims of the current, half-equality between the sexes – but in an active, self-respecting partnership with men. By so doing, women will develop confidence in their own ability to determine actively, in partnership with men, the conditions of their life, their choices, their future and their society.

"OH LIBERTY!"
Marie-Jeanne Roland de la Platière

Chiefly remembered now for the phrase below, which she murmured to the clay statue of Liberty in the Place de la Revolution just before she was guillotined, Madame de Roland had been a popular hostess with the leaders of the Revolution, who often met at her salon. She was influential behind the scenes, working with her husband who was a leading revolutionary and rose to become Minister for the Interior. However, after he spoke out against the Revolution's slide into violence, they were both in danger and imprisoned. He managed to escape beyond the reaches of the revolutionary guard, but when he learned of her execution in November 1793, he killed himself.

O Liberté, que de crimes on commet en ton nom!
(Oh Liberty, what crimes are committed in thy name!)

"NO MAN HAS THE RIGHT TO FIX THE BOUNDARY TO THE MARCH OF A NATION"
Charles Stewart Parnell

Charles Stewart Parnell was one of the most charismatic politicians of his day, an ardent advocate of Irish Home Rule and widely admired even by politicans who disagreed with his ideals. He had earlier campaigned for the three fs – fair rent, fixity of tenure and freedom of sale – and achieved qualified success. This speech, given in Cork during the lead-up to the general election campaign of 1885, indicates the terms he would accept and those he would not. One of his greatest achievements was to bring together several disparate parties within the Home Rule movement and mould them into a modern political party, thus giving them a much more effective voice.

At the election in 1880 I laid certain principles before you and you accepted them. I said and I pledged myself, that I should form one of an independent Irish party to act in opposition to every English government which refused to concede the just rights of Ireland. And the longer time which is gone by since then, the more I am convinced that that is the true policy to pursue so far as parliamentary policy is concerned, and that it will be impossible for either or both of the English parties to contend for any long time against a determined band of Irishmen acting honestly upon these principles, and backed by the Irish people . . .

Nobody could point to any single action of ours in the House of Commons or out of it which was not based upon the knowledge that behind us existed a strong and brave people, that without the help of the people our exertions would be as nothing, and that with their help and with their confidence we should be, as I believe we shall prove to be in the near future, invincible and unconquerable.

We shall struggle, as we have been struggling, for the great and important interests of the Irish tenant farmer. We shall ask that his industry shall not be fettered by rent. We shall ask also from the farmer in return that he shall do what in him lies to encourage the struggling manufactures of Ireland, and that he shall not think it too great a sacrifice to be called upon when he wants anything, when he has to purchase anything, to consider how he may get it of Irish material and manufacture, even supposing he has to pay a little more for it. I am sorry if the agricultural population has shown itself somewhat deficient in its sense of duty in this respect up to the present time, but I feel convinced that the matter has only to be put before them to secure the opening up of most important markets in this country for those manufactures which have always existed, and for those which have been reopened anew, as a consequence of the recent exhibitions, the great exhibition in Dublin and the other equally great one in Cork, which have been recently held.

We shall also endeavour to secure for the labourer some recognition and some right in the land of his country. We don't care whether it be the prejudices of the farmer or of the landlord that stands in his way. We consider that whatever class tries to obstruct the labourer in the possession of those fair and just rights to which he is entitled, that class should be put down, and coerced if you will, into doing justice to the labourer . . .

Well, but gentlemen, I go back from the consideration of these questions to the land question, in which the labourers' question is also involved and the manufacturers' question. I come back – and every Irish politician must be forcibly driven back – to the consideration of the great question of national self-government for Ireland. I do not know how this great question will be eventually settled. I do not know whether England will be wise in time and concede to constitutional arguments and methods the restitution of that which was stolen from us towards the close of the last century. It is given to none of us to forecast the future, and just as it is impossible for us to say in what way or by what means the national question may be settled, in what way full justice may be done to Ireland, so it is impossible for us to say to what extent that justice should be done. We cannot ask for less than restitution of Grattan's Parliament. But no man has the right to fix the boundary to the march of a nation. No man has a right to say to his country: 'Thus far shalt thou go, and no further'; and we have never attempted to fix the *ne plus ultra* to the progress of Ireland's nationhood, and we never shall.

But gentlemen, while we leave those things to time, circumstances, and the future, we must each one of us resolve in our own hearts that we shall at all times do everything which within us lies to obtain for Ireland the fullest measure of her rights. In this way we shall avoid difficulties and contentions amongst each other. In this way we shall not give up anything which the future may put in favour of our country, and while we struggle today for that which may seem possible for us with our combination, we must struggle for it with the proud consciousness, and that we shall not do anything to hinder or prevent better men who may come after us from gaining better things than those for which we now contend.

"THE RIGHT TO EXIST"
Menachem Begin

Having won the general election in May, Menachem Begin took office as Prime Minister of Israel on 20 June, 1977. Earlier in the day he had been to the Western Wall to pray and had conducted an impromptu question-and-answer session with members of the international press corps nearby. A large number of the questions were about his plans for relations with the PLO. One reporter needled him by asking him for his response to Yassir Arafat's assertion that the Jewish state had no right of existence. His acceptance speech at the Knesset had acquired a last-minute addition. After a measured description of how Likud had come to beat Labour, he changed tone and thundered:

The right to exist? Would it enter the mind of any Briton or Frenchman, Belgian or Dutchman, Hungarian or Bulgarian, Russian or American, to request for its people recognition of its right to exist? Their existence per se is their right to exist!

We were granted our right to exist by the God of our fathers at the glimmer of the dawn of human civilization 4,000 years ago.

And so it is that the Jewish people have a historic, eternal and inalienable right to Eretz Yisrael, the land of our forefathers. And for that right, which has been sanctified in Jewish blood from generation to generation, we have paid a price unexemplified in the annals of the nations.

"ADDRESS TO IRISH IMMIGRANTS"
George Washington

Less than three months after the signature of the treaty that ended the Revolutionary Wars, George Washington addressed a group of Irish immigrants who had recently arrived in New York. For the next few years he retired to his plantation at Mount Vernon. He re-entered politics in 1787, to preside over the Philadelpia Convention that drafted the Constitution of the United States of America and become the first President of the USA in 1789. In fact, immigration did not increase markedly until the 1830s, but from then on it grew rapidly. Irish people, especially, came to work in the industries that were springing up in American cities.

Gentlemen: The testimony of your satisfaction at the glorious termination of the late contest, and your indulgent opinion of my Agency in it, affords me singular pleasure and merits my warmest acknowledgment.

If the Example of the Americans successfully contending in the Cause of Freedom, can be of any use to other Nations; we shall have an additional Motive for rejoycing at so prosperous an Event. It was not an uninteresting consideration to learn that the Kingdom of Ireland, by a bold and manly conduct, had obtained the redress of many of its grievances; and it is much to be wished that the blessings of equal Liberty and unrestrained Commerce may yet prevail more extensively; in the mean time, you may be assured, Gentlemen, that the Hospitality and Beneficence of your Countrymen, to our Brethren who have been Prisoners of War, are neither unknown, or unregarded.

The bosom of America is open to receive not only the Opulent and respectable Stranger, but the oppressed and persecuted of all Nations And Religions; whom we shall welcome to a participation of all our rights and privileges, if by decency and propriety of conduct they appear to merit the enjoyment.

"OUR TIME HAS COME"
Jesse Jackson

The Reverend Jesse Jackson is one of the best-known civil-rights activists in the USA and a long-standing senior figure in the Democrat Party. He stood for nomination as Democrat presidential candidate in both 1984 and 1988. During the 1960s he participated in the Southern Christian Leadership Conference and was national director of its Operation Breadbasket and later extended his efforts into international affairs. In 1984, he came third behind Gary Hart and former Vice President Walter Mondale. In his speech at the Convention he called on the delegates to unite, whatever the colour of their skin, to eradicate injustice, division, racism and poverty.

Thank you very much.

Tonight we come together bound by our faith in a mighty God, with genuine respect and love for our country, and inheriting the legacy of a great Party, the Democratic Party, which is the best hope for redirecting our nation on a more humane, just, and peaceful course . . .

. . . Our time has come. Our time has come. Suffering breeds character. Character breeds faith. In the end, faith will not disappoint. Our time has come. Our faith, hope, and dreams will prevail. Our time has come. Weeping has endured for nights, but now joy cometh in the morning. Our time has come. No grave can hold our body down. Our time has come. No lie can live forever. Our time has come. We must leave racial battle ground and come to economic common ground and moral higher ground. America, our time has come. We come from disgrace to amazing grace. Our time has come. Give me your tired, give me your poor, your huddled masses who yearn to breathe free and come November, there will be a change because our time has come.

"PARKS' BUS PROTEST"
Rosa Parks

On 1 December, 1955, in Montgomery, Alabama the local secretary of the National Association for the Advancement of Colored People, Rosa Parks, defied a bus driver who ordered her to give up her seat to a white man. He threatened to get the police to arrest her and she answered as below. In March, a 15-year-old schoolgirl, Claudette Colvin, had been arrested for the same action. On the day of Parks' trial, the Montgomery Bus Boycott, in which virtually all African American passengers found other means of getting around the city, started. It lasted for 381 days and ended only with the repeal of the law requiring segregation on buses.

You may go on and do so.

"THE RIGHT TO SAY WHAT YOU SAY"
Voltaire

This remark is widely attributed to Voltaire, but its source has not been proved. The first definite appearance is in a 1906 book about Voltaire by Evelyn Beatrice Hall (writing under the pseudonym Stephen G. Tallentyre), in which she sums up his ideas on free thought. A similar idea appears in a remark by Voltaire about the author of *de l'Esprit* (*On the Mind*), Claude Adrien Helvétius, who claimed in his book that humans are no different morally from animals. Voltaire commented, 'This man was worth more than all his enemies together, but I never approved of either the errors in his book nor the trivial truths that he produces with such emphasis. I took his part openly when absurd men condemned him for the truths.'

I disapprove of what you say, but I will defend to the death your right to say it.

"I BELIEVE IN VOTES FOR WOMEN"
Women's Social and Political Union (WSPU)

This mock creed for the Women's Social and Political Union (WSPU) is a parody on the Christian creed. By the time this was written, Christabel Pankhurst had already served two terms in prison for disorder. After a third term she went to live in Paris. On her return to Britain in 1913, she was re-arrested under the Prisoners (Temporary Discharge for Ill Health) Act 1913. This had replaced the earlier practice of force-feeding hunger strikers with a regime under which they would be allowed to starve themselves, then be released on grounds of ill health when too weak to protest, and then re-arrested for the most trivial of transgressions. Christabel served three months of her three-year sentence before being released.

I believe in Emmeline Pankhurst – Founder of the Women's Social and Political Union. And in Christabel Pankhurst, her eldest daughter, Our Lady, who was inspired by the Passion for Liberty – born to be a leader of women. Suffered under Liberal Government, was arrested, tried and sentenced. She descended into prison; the seventh day she returned again to the world. She was entertained to breakfast, and sat on the right hand of her mother, our glorious Leader, from thence she went forth to judge both the government and the Antis. I believe in Votes for Women on the same terms as men, the policy of the Women's Social and Political Union, the equality of the sexes, Representation for Taxation, the necessity for militant tactics, and Freedom Everlasting. Amen!

"UNREST IN SOUTH AFRICA"
Desmond Tutu

When the then Bishop of Johannesburg, Desmond Tutu – later
Anglican Archbishop of Cape Town – gave the warning below to
South African Prime Minister Johannes Vorster, he was talking
about general unrest among the black majority in the country,
but what triggered the Soweto Uprising three weeks later was
a ruling that certain lessons in black schools had to be taught
in Afrikaans, a language the black majority associated with the
apartheid regime and oppression. Thousands of schoolchildren
walked out of their schools and in the ensuing chaos 23 people
were killed. According to the highest estimates as many as 600
people died in the following days.

Unless something drastic is done very soon, then bloodshed and
violence are going to happen . . . A people made desperate by
despair and injustice and oppressions will use desperate means.

"A WOMAN WITHOUT A MAN"
Gloria Steinem

This slightly surreal saying – a response to the idea that a woman without a man is incomplete and unfulfilled – has long been attributed to feminist icon Steinem, although there is little proof, except that she was editor of *Ms* magazine when the t-shirts with the slogan appeared. The magazine first appeared in July 1972, a year after she had co-founded the grassroots National Women's Political Caucus to address the issues of reproductive freedom, the passage of the Equal Rights Amendment and affordable childcare. Other groups she founded or has been deeply involved with include the Women's Action Alliance, the Democratic Socialists of America and Choice USA.

A woman without a man is like a fish without a bicycle.

"PRESIDENTIAL ACCEPTANCE SPEECH"
Barack Obama

On 4 November, 2008 after what earlier in the year had seemed like an unlikely victory, Senator Barack Obama won the Presidential election by 52.5 to 42.7 per cent of votes cast. His acceptance speech at Grant Park Stadium late in the evening was watched by some 240,000 people, and millions more all round the world. In it, he thanked all the people who had helped with or donated to the campaign, set out his future plans in broad brush-strokes and referenced Presidents Lincoln and Kennedy, as well as Dr Martin Luther King.

If there is anyone out there who still doubts that America is a place where all things are possible; who still wonders if the dream of our founders is alive in our time; who still questions the power of our democracy, tonight is your answer . . .

. . . Where we are met with cynicism and doubt, and those who tell us that we can't, we will respond with that timeless creed that sums up the spirit of a people: yes, we can.

SPORT

"WINNING ISN'T EVERYTHING . . ."
Vincent Thomas Lombardi

Vince Lombardi, head coach of the Green Bay Packers from
1959 to 1967, is the best-known of the various people to whom
this maxim is attributed – although he claimed that he was
misquoted and said it was the will to win that was the only thing.
Whatever he actually said, it certainly had the desired effect.
During his eight-year tenure at the Lambreau Field, his intensive
training methods and expectation of complete dedication from
his players turned the Packers from an under-performing side
to one that won five NFL league championships (including three
in a row in 1965, 1966 and 1967) and the first two Superbowls.
The maxim was taken up by other sporting institutions across
America and beyond.

Winning isn't everything: it's the only thing.

"DESCENDING EVEREST"
Sir Edmund Hillary

After Edmund Hillary and Tenzing Norgay had reached the summit of Mount Everest early on 29 May, 1953 Hillary took several photographs to prove that they had done so and after 15 minutes they rapidly made their way back down. Part-way back down to camp, they were greeted by Hillary's life-long friend George Lowe with some hot soup. Lowe responded to Hillary's comment, below, with a cheery 'Thought you must have.'. This assault on Everest, led by British mountaineer John Hunt, was Hillary's second to the mountain and Tenzing Norgay's seventh. The names of the two successful climbers, Hunt and those who helped them near the summit are well known, but the expedition actually had a complement of 400.

Well, we knocked the bastard off!

"KEEP COMING BACK"
Grantland Rice

Grantland Rice was one of the greatest sports journalists of the twentieth century, writing articles that covered events in the careers of such stars as Babe Ruth, Jack Dempsey and Knute Rockne. This is the last verse of his poem about the struggles for success and glory – both on and off the field – of an aspiring American football player called Bill Jones.

Keep coming back, and though the world may romp across your spine,
Let every game's end find you still upon the battling line;
For when the One Great Scorer comes to mark against your name,
He writes – not that you won or lost – but how you played the Game.

"IT'S ALL RIGHT. I'M NOT AFRAID"
George 'Gipper' Gipp

Even nearly 90 years after his early death, George Gipp is still remembered as one of the most talented college football players ever, but it is perhaps as the author of coach Knute Rockne's 'Win one for the Gipper' exhortation that he is best known. Rockne used the phrase for years after Gipp's early death at the age of 25, saying that the words had been said to him by the star footballer on his deathbed. The – possibly apocryphal – story is that Gipp had been used to getting back to his college after hours and letting himself in through a stage door to the campus theatre. On one occasion it was locked and, rather than try to get in by another way, he stayed out in the cold. He contracted a streptococcal infection and died within a few days.

I've got to go, Rock. It's all right. I'm not afraid. Some time, Rock, when the team is up against it, when things are wrong and the breaks are beating the boys, ask them to go in there with all they've got and win just one for the Gipper. I don't know where I'll be then, Rock. But I'll know about it, and I'll be happy.

"JACOBS VS SHARKEY"
Joe Jacobs

In 1929 the German heavyweight champion boxer, Max
Schmeling, visited America and acquired a new manager, fast-
talking New Yorker Joe Jacobs, who promoted him tirelessly.
In 1930 Schmeling got his first attempt at the recently vacated
World Heavyweight title, against Jack Sharkey. He won the bout
after Sharkey was disqualified for landing a low blow. Two years
later a rematch was arranged, and Sharkey won a highly
disputed points victory that people who witnessed the fight said
was the worst judging decision ever made. Of course Jacobs was
absolutely furious and grabbed a microphone, yelling angrily in
his heavy East-European accent. The pair remained associates
for most of the rest of the decade, even in the face of the German
Minister of Sport instructing Schmeling to spend more time in
Europe and drop his association with Jacobs and other Jewish
associates, an order that the champion had the courage to
ignore.

We was robbed!

"A LONG WAY FROM 143rd STREET"
Althea Gibson

Althea Gibson, who came from a troubled background in New York's Harlem, was the first African American to win a tennis Grand Slam tournament: in fact, she won five – the French Open in 1956 and Wimbledon and the US Open in both 1957 and 1958. It was only in 1950, aged 23, that she was allowed to compete in the US Open as until then lawn tennis was still basically a segregated sport, until an article by Alice Marble in the *American Lawn Tennis* magazine pointed out that to exclude her on grounds of colour was sanctimonious hypocrisy.

It seemed a long way from 143rd Street. Shaking hands with the Queen of England was a long way from being forced to sit in the colored section of the bus going into downtown Wilmington, North Carolina. Dancing with the Duke of Devonshire was a long way from not being allowed to bowl in Jefferson City, Missouri, because the white customers complained about it.

"THE TAKING PART, NOT THE WINNING, IS THE IMPORTANT THING"
Baron de Coubertin (Pierre de Frédy)

The first Modern Olympiad was held in Athens in 1896. The fourth Olympiad was held in London, and the perceived over-excitement of some competitors led the Bishop of Philadelphia to remind them in a sermon that taking part was more important than winning. The founder of the games, de Courbertin, repeated the idea in the words below at an official banquet on 24 July, 1908 as a philsophy of life. The idea first came into widespread prominence in 1932 when it appeared at the opening ceremony of the Los Angeles Games as 'The important thing in the Olympic Games is not winning but taking part. The essential thing is not conquering but fighting well.' Its current form was established at the 1936 Berlin Olympics, when a recording of de Courbertin was played, saying *'L'important aux Jeux Olympiques n'est pas d'y gagner mais d'y prendre part car l'essentiel dans la vie ce n'est pas tout de conquérir que de bien lutter.'* 'The important thing in the Olympic Games is not winning but taking part for the essential thing in life is not conquering but fighting well.'

The important thing in life is not the triumph but the struggle, the essential thing is not to have conquered but to have fought well.

"FURTHER TO FALL"
Bob Fitzsimmons

Fitzsimmons started his professional boxing career in Australia in the early 1880s, having boxed as an amateur in New Zealand. He had immense punching power as a result of years spent helping in his blacksmith brother's forge as a youngster. He moved to America in 1890 in search of better money, becoming World Middleweight Champion in 1891 and World Heavyweight Champion in 1897. The response, below, to a question about how he felt about fighting a man larger than himself was not prophetic. On 9 June, 1899 the taller and heavier James Jeffries knocked him out in the eleventh round.

The bigger they are, the further they have to fall.

POLITICS

"THE DECLARATION OF INDEPENDENCE"
Thomas Jefferson

One year into the American Revolutionary War, delegates to the Second Continental Congress voted on 2 July, 1776 to declare independence from the British Crown. Two days later, the text – designed to explain to the population why Congress had voted for independence – was finalized then printed and distributed. In the preceding decade, the British Crown had increased taxation on its colonies to pay off its vast national debt and laws had been passed by the British Parliament to increase its control over the colonies, leading some to question whether it had violated the latter's rights and therefore its own right to rule.

When, in the course of human events, it becomes necessary for one people to dissolve the political bonds which have connected them with another, and to assume among the powers of the earth, the separate and equal station to which the laws of nature and of nature's God entitle them, a decent respect to the opinions of mankind requires that they should declare the causes which impel them to the separation.

We hold these truths to be self-evident, that all men are created equal, that they are endowed by their Creator with certain unalienable rights, that among these are life, liberty and the pursuit of happiness. That to secure these rights, governments are instituted among men, deriving their just powers from the consent of the governed. That whenever any form of government becomes destructive to these ends, it is the right of the people to alter or to abolish it, and to institute new government, laying its foundation on such principles and organizing its powers in such form, as to them shall seem most likely to effect their safety and happiness. Prudence, indeed, will dictate that governments long established should not be changed for light and transient causes; and accordingly all experience hath shown that mankind are more disposed to suffer, while evils are sufferable, than to right themselves by abolishing the forms to which they are accustomed. But when a long train of abuses and usurpations, pursuing invariably the same object evinces a design to reduce them under absolute despotism, it is their right, it is their duty, to throw off such government, and to provide new guards for their future security. Such has been the patient sufferance of these colonies; and such is now the necessity which constrains them to alter their former systems of government. The history of the present King of Great Britain is a history of repeated injuries and usurpations, all having in direct object the establishment of an absolute tyranny over these states. To prove this, let facts be submitted to a candid world.

He has refused his assent to laws, the most wholesome and necessary for the public good.

He has forbidden his governors to pass laws of immediate and pressing importance, unless suspended in their operation till his assent should be obtained; and when so suspended, he has utterly neglected to attend to them.

He has refused to pass other laws for the accommodation of large districts of people, unless those people would relinquish the right of representation in the legislature, a right inestimable to them and formidable to tyrants only.

He has called together legislative bodies at places unusual, uncomfortable, and distant from the depository of their public records, for the sole purpose of fatiguing them into compliance with his measures.

He has dissolved representative houses repeatedly, for opposing with manly firmness his invasions on the rights of the people.

He has refused for a long time, after such dissolutions, to cause others to be elected; whereby the legislative powers, incapable of annihilation, have returned to the people at large for their exercise; the state remaining in the meantime exposed to all the dangers of invasion from without, and convulsions within.

He has endeavored to prevent the population of these states; for that purpose obstructing the laws for naturalization of foreigners; refusing to pass others to encourage their migration hither, and raising the conditions of new appropriations of lands.

He has obstructed the administration of justice, by refusing his assent to laws for establishing judiciary powers.

He has made judges dependent on his will alone, for the tenure of their offices, and the amount and payment of their salaries.

He has erected a multitude of new offices, and sent hither swarms of officers to harass our people, and eat out their substance.

He has kept among us, in times of peace, standing armies without the consent of our legislature.

He has affected to render the military independent of and superior to civil power.

He has combined with others to subject us to a jurisdiction foreign to our constitution, and unacknowledged by our laws; giving his assent to their acts of pretended legislation:

For quartering large bodies of armed troops among us:

For protecting them, by mock trial, from punishment for any murders which they should commit on the inhabitants of these states:

For cutting off our trade with all parts of the world:

For imposing taxes on us without our consent:

For depriving us in many cases, of the benefits of trial by jury:

For transporting us beyond seas to be tried for pretended offenses:

For abolishing the free system of English laws in a neighbouring province, establishing therein an arbitrary government, and enlarging its boundaries so as to render it at once an example and fit instrument for introducing the same absolute rule in these colonies:

For taking away our charters, abolishing our most valuable laws, and altering fundamentally the forms of our governments:

For suspending our own legislatures, and declaring themselves invested with power to legislate for us in all cases whatsoever.

He has abdicated government here, by declaring us out of his protection and waging war against us.

He has plundered our seas, ravaged our coasts, burned our towns, and destroyed the lives of our people.

He is at this time transporting large armies of foreign mercenaries to complete the works of death, desolation and tyranny, already begun with circumstances of cruelty and perfidy scarcely paralleled in the most barbarous ages, and totally unworthy the head of a civilized nation.

He has constrained our fellow citizens taken captive on the high seas to bear arms against their country, to become the executioners of their friends and brethren, or to fall themselves by their hands.

He has excited domestic insurrections amongst us, and has endeavored to bring on the inhabitants of our frontiers, the merciless Indian savages, whose known rule of warfare, is undistinguished destruction of all ages, sexes and conditions.

In every stage of these oppressions we have petitioned for redress in the most humble terms: our repeated petitions have been answered only by repeated injury. A prince, whose character is thus marked by every act which may define a tyrant, is unfit to be the ruler of a free people.

Nor have we been wanting in attention to our British brethren. We have warned them from time to time of attempts by their legislature to extend an unwarrantable jurisdiction over us. We have reminded them of the circumstances of our emigration and settlement here. We have appealed to their native justice and magnanimity, and we have conjured them by the ties of our common kindred to disavow these usurpations, which, would inevitably interrupt our connections and correspondence. They too have been deaf to the voice of justice and of consanguinity. We must, therefore, acquiesce in the necessity, which denounces our separation, and hold them, as we hold the rest of mankind,

enemies in war, in peace friends.

We, therefore, the representatives of the United States of America, in General Congress, assembled, appealing to the Supreme Judge of the world for the rectitude of our intentions, do, in the name, and by the authority of the good people of these colonies, solemnly publish and declare, that these united colonies are, and of right ought to be free and independent states; that they are absolved from all allegiance to the British Crown, and that all political connection between them and the state of Great Britain, is and ought to be totally dissolved; and that as free and independent states, they have full power to levy war, conclude peace, contract alliances, establish commerce, and to do all other acts and things which independent states may of right do. And for the support of this declaration, with a firm reliance on the protection of Divine Providence, we mutually pledge to each other our lives, our fortunes and our sacred honour.

"IF IT AIN'T BROKE . . ."
Bert Lance (Thomas Bertram)

Bert Lance was a businessman and Democrat politician. As President Carter's director of the Office of the Budget and Management, he saw part of his role as saving the government billions of dollars through a policy of non-intervention in departments and systems that were working well enough, as throwing money at them will not increase their efficiency significantly. It has become something of a motto for politicans who believe in pared-down government. Soon after taking on his role in government, Lance was accused of corruption and mismanagement while on the board of Calhoun National Bank. He was forced to resign but was subsequently acquitted

If it ain't broke, don't fix it.

"BETTER RED . . ."
Bertrand Russell

During World War II Joseph Goebbels, one of Hitler's closest
associates, coined the term 'Better dead than Red' against the
Russian regime, and this was either adopted or reinvented by
McCarthyites during the 1950s. As a retort, the British
philosopher Bertrand Russell posited that at an extreme level,
the opposite was true. This became sloganized as below, and was
adopted by the British Campaign for Nuclear Disarmament,
whose members argued not that they wanted to be communists
but that unilateral disarmament was preferable to nuclear war.
Interestingly, it was also used by those against disarmament to
ridicule them. President Kennedy criticized both points of view
as too extreme.

Better Red than dead.

"BETTER A LION THAN A SHEEP"
Benito Mussolini

This adage, adopted by Mussolini, became one of the most
popular Fascist slogans in Italy, epitomizing the Fascist ideal. He
had formed the Italian Fascists in 1919, and in its early years the
movement gained widespread popularity because it created a
vision of an Italy restored to the glories of the Roman Empire
and opposed any form of class warfare – something that many
in Europe feared as they learned of the horrors of the Russian
Revolution. He took control of the Italian Parliament in a coup
in 1922 after King Vittorio Emanuele III took the pragmatic
decision to support him, given that he had the backing of the
army. He went on to create a police state, with a confused
political ideology that incorporated aspects of anticommunism,
anticapitalism, antiliberalism, totalitarianism and nationalism.

It is better to have lived one day as a lion than one hundred years
as a sheep.

"AT KARL MARX'S FUNERAL"
Friedrich Engels

Although less famous now than Karl Marx, Engels was
instrumental in developing communist theory and was co-author
of *The Communist Manifesto* (1848). He already had radical
leanings as a student which his father, a wealthy manufacturer,
disapproved of intensely and he was sent to England to get
some work experience. But the horrific working conditions
– particularly of women and children – radicalized him even
further. He and Marx remained close collaborators for almost 40
years, and he even went back to work at the hated Manchester
factory in order to be able to support Marx financially. At Marx's
funeral, Engels spoke movingly of his friend's life and work.

On the 14th of March, at a quarter to three in the afternoon, the
greatest living thinker ceased to think. He had been left alone for
scarcely two minutes, and when we came back we found him in his
armchair, peacefully gone to sleep-but forever.

An immeasurable loss has been sustained both by the militant
proletariat of Europe and America, and by historical science, in the
death of this man. The gap that has been left by the departure of
this mighty spirit will soon enough make itself felt.

Just as Darwin discovered the law of development of organic
nature, so Marx discovered the law of development of human
history: the simple fact, hitherto concealed by an overgrowth of
ideology, that mankind must first of all eat, drink, have shelter and
clothing, before it can pursue politics, science, art, religion, etc.;
that therefore the production of the immediate material means of
subsistence and consequently the degree of economic development
attained by a given people or during a given epoch form
the foundation upon which the state institutions, the legal
conceptions, art, and even the ideas on religion, of the people
concerned have been evolved, and in the light of which they must,

therefore, be explained, instead of vice versa, as had hitherto been the case.

But that is not all. Marx also discovered the special law of motion governing the present-day capitalist mode of production and the bourgeois society that this mode of production has created. The discovery of surplus value suddenly threw light on the problem, in trying to solve which all previous investigations, of both bourgeois economists and socialist critics, had been groping in the dark.

Two such discoveries would be enough for one lifetime. Happy the man to whom it is granted to make even one such discovery. But in every single field which Marx investigated – and he investigated very many fields, none of them superficially – in every field, even in that of mathematics, he made independent discoveries.

Such was the man of science. But this was not even half the man. Science was for Marx a historically dynamic, revolutionary force. However great the joy with which he welcomed a new discovery in some theoretical science whose practical application perhaps it was as yet quite impossible to envisage, he experienced quite another kind of joy when the discovery involved immediate revolutionary changes in industry and in historical development in general. For example, he followed closely the development of the discoveries made in the field of electricity and recently those of Marcel Deprez.

For Marx was before all else a revolutionist. His real mission in life was to contribute, in one way or another, to the overthrow of capitalist society and of the state institutions which it had brought into being, to contribute to the liberation of the modern proletariat, which he was the first to make conscious of its own position and its needs, conscious of the conditions of its emancipation. Fighting was his element. And he fought with a passion, a tenacity and a success such as few could rival. His work on the first *Rheinische Zeitung* (1842), the *Paris Vorwärts!* (1844), *Brüsseler Deutsche Zeitung* (1847), the *Neue Rheinische Zeitung* (1848-49), the *New York Tribune* (1852-61), and in addition to these a host of militant pamphlets, work in organisations in Paris, Brussels and London, and finally, crowning all, the formation of the great International Working Men's Association – this was indeed an achievement of which its founder might well have been proud even if he had done nothing else.

And, consequently, Marx was the best-hated and most calumniated man of his time. Governments, both absolutist and republican, deported him from their territories. Bourgeois, whether conservative or ultrademocratic, vied with one another in heaping slanders upon him. All this he brushed aside as though it were cobweb, ignoring it, answering only when extreme necessity compelled him. And he died beloved, revered and mourned by millions of revolutionary fellow-workers – from the mines of Siberia to California, in all parts of Europe and America – and I make bold to say that though he may have had many opponents he had hardly one personal enemy.

His name will endure through the ages, and so will his work!

"THE NEW DEAL"
Franklin D. Roosevelt

In 1933 America was in the depths of the Great Depression that had followed the Wall Street Crash of 1929. Franklin D. Roosevelt formulated a detailed plan to revitalize the US economy, help the urban and – particularly – rural poor and the unemployed, whilst also reforming the financial institutions whose irresponsibility had caused the mess. This imaginative plan was known as the New Deal. In his first inaugural address in March 1933, Roosevelt laid the blame at the feet of financiers, bankers, profit-seeking and capitalism's overwhelming self-interest, sentiments echoed in another inaugural address almost 76 years later.

This is a day of national consecration. And I am certain that on this day my fellow Americans expect that on my induction into the Presidency, I will address them with a candour and a decision which the present situation of our people impels.

This is preeminently the time to speak the truth, the whole truth, frankly and boldly. Nor need we shrink from honestly facing conditions in our country today. This great Nation will endure, as it has endured, will revive and will prosper.

So, first of all, let me assert my firm belief that the only thing we have to fear is fear itself – nameless, unreasoning, unjustified terror which paralyzes needed efforts to convert retreat into advance. In every dark hour of our national life, a leadership of frankness and of vigor has met with that understanding and support of the people themselves which is essential to victory. And I am convinced that you will again give that support to leadership in these critical days . . .

. . . The rulers of the exchange of mankind's goods have failed, through their own stubbornness and their own incompetence, have admitted their failure, and have abdicated. Practices of the unscrupulous money changers stand indicted in the court of public opinion, rejected by the hearts and minds of men . . .

Yes, the money changers have fled from their high seats in the temple of our civilization. We may now restore that temple to the ancient truths. The measure of that restoration lies in the extent to which we apply social values more noble than mere monetary profit.

Happiness lies not in the mere possession of money; it lies in the joy of achievement, in the thrill of creative effort. The joy, the moral stimulation of work no longer must be forgotten in the mad chase of evanescent profits. These dark days, my friends, will be worth all they cost us if they teach us that our true destiny is not to be ministered unto but to minister to ourselves, to our fellow men.

Recognition of that falsity of material wealth as the standard of success goes hand in hand with the abandonment of the false belief that public office and high political position are to be valued only by the standards of pride of place and personal profit; and there must be an end to a conduct in banking and in business which too often has given to a sacred trust the likeness of callous and selfish wrongdoing. Small wonder that confidence languishes, for it thrives only on honesty, on honour, on the sacredness of obligations, on faithful protection, and on unselfish performance; without them it cannot live.

Restoration calls, however, not for changes in ethics alone. This nation is asking for action, and action now.

Our greatest primary task is to put people to work. This is no unsolvable problem if we face it wisely and courageously. It can be accomplished in part by direct recruiting by the Government itself, treating the task as we would treat the emergency of a war, but at the same time, through this employment, accomplishing great – greatly needed projects to stimulate and reorganize the use of our great natural resources . . .

Yes, the task can be helped by definite efforts to raise the values of agricultural products, and with this the power to purchase the output of our cities. It can be helped by preventing realistically the tragedy of the growing loss through foreclosure of our small homes and our farms. It can be helped by insistence that the Federal, the State, and the local governments act forthwith on the demand that their cost be drastically reduced. It can be helped by the unifying of relief activities which today are often scattered, uneconomical, unequal. It can be helped by national planning for and supervision of all forms of transportation and of communications and other utilities that have a definitely public character. There are many ways in which it can be helped, but it can never be helped by merely talking about it . . .

And finally, in our progress towards a resumption of work, we require two safeguards against a return of the evils of the old order. There must be a strict supervision of all banking and credits and investments. There must be an end to speculation with other people's money. And there must be provision for an adequate but sound currency . . .

Through this program of action we address ourselves to putting our own national house in order and making income balance outgo. Our international trade relations, though vastly important, are in point of time, and necessity, secondary to the establishment of a sound national economy. I favor, as a practical policy, the putting of first things first. I shall spare no effort to restore world trade by international economic readjustment; but the emergency at home cannot wait on that accomplishment.

The basic thought that guides these specific means of national recovery is not nationally – narrowly nationalistic. It is the insistence, as a first consideration, upon the interdependence of the various elements in and parts of the United States of America – a recognition of the old and permanently important manifestation of the American spirit of the pioneer. It is the way to recovery. It is the immediate way. It is the strongest assurance that recovery will endure.

In the field of world policy, I would dedicate this Nation to the policy of the good neighbour: the neighbour who resolutely respects himself and, because he does so, respects the rights of others; the neighbour who respects his obligations and respects the sanctity of his agreements in and with a world of neighbours . . .

We are, I know, ready and willing to submit our lives and our property to such discipline, because it makes possible a leadership which aims at the larger good. This, I propose to offer, pledging that the larger purposes will bind upon us, bind upon us all as a sacred obligation with a unity of duty hitherto evoked only in times of armed strife.

With this pledge taken, I assume unhesitatingly the leadership of this great army of our people dedicated to a disciplined attack upon our common problems.

Action in this image, action to this end is feasible under the form of government which we have inherited from our ancestors. Our Constitution is so simple, so practical that it is possible always to meet extraordinary needs by changes in emphasis and arrangement without loss of essential form. That is why our constitutional system has proved itself the most superbly enduring political mechanism the modern world has ever seen.

It has met every stress of vast expansion of territory, of foreign wars, of bitter internal strife, of world relations. And it is to be hoped that the normal balance of executive and legislative authority may be wholly equal, wholly adequate to meet the unprecedented task before us. But it may be that an unprecedented demand and need for undelayed action may call for temporary departure from that normal balance of public procedure.

I am prepared under my constitutional duty to recommend the measures that a stricken nation in the midst of a stricken world may require. These measures, or such other measures as the Congress may build out of its experience and wisdom, I shall seek, within my constitutional authority, to bring to speedy adoption . . .

For the trust reposed in me, I will return the courage and the devotion that befit the time. I can do no less . . .

In this dedication – In this dedication of a Nation, we humbly ask the blessing of God.

May He protect each and every one of us.

May He guide me in the days to come.

"CALL TO THE REPUBLICANS"
Charles Baudelaire

At the end of 1851 Napoleon III had retaken France, ending the Second Republic. During the next decade his autocratic rule, suppression of press freedom, assumption of executive power, censorship and surveillance of individuals rankled with French citizens used to greater liberty. He started loosening restrictions in the early 1860s, but not sufficiently quickly for the disgruntled working classes who – won over by the collectivist theories of Marx and Mikhail Bakunin – launched strikes and mass protests. Baudelaire's clarion call to the Republicans catches the temper of the time and presages the violence, destruction and anarchy that would come with the short-lived revolutionary Paris Commune of 1871.

When I agree to be a Republican, I commit evil knowingly. Yes! Long Live Revolution. I am not a dupe! I was never a dupe! I say Long live Revolution! as I would say Long Live Destruction! Long Live Expiation! Long Live Punishment! Long Live Death!

"CONDITIONS FOR ABDICATION"
Senate of Nanking

After the successful Xinhai Revolution of 1911, on 6 February, 1912 the Senate of Nanking passed a resolution for the Imperial Edict for Abdication. The prequistite conditions for abdication included the list below. After negotiations between President Li Huanhung and the Dowager Empress Longyu, it was agreed that the five-year-old emperor would abdicate, according to these terms, with a few minor variations. She signed the edict on 12 February and it was proclaimed from Beijing's Tiananmen Gate. He would remain in the Forbidden City until 1924. In 1932 he was installed as puppet king in Japanese-controlled Manchukuo (formerly Manchuria) and abdicated again at the end of World War II.

* The Qing Emperor remains and will be treated as a foreign monarch by the Republic Government.
* The Republic will allocate 4,000,000 Yuan each year for royal expenses.
* The emperor will remain in the Forbidden City until he can be transferred to Yeheyuan.
* Royal temple and tombs will be guarded and maintained.
* The expenses of Guangxu's tomb will be disbursed by the Republic.
* Royal employees will remain in the Forbidden City with the exception of eunuchs.
* Private property of the royal family will be protected by the Republic.
* Royal forces will be incorporated into the army of the Republic.

"WE MUST DEFEND THE COUNTRY"
Mustafa Kemel Atatürk

The Ottoman Empire had joined the Axis Powers during World War I and had suffered defeat. While the Allies were deciding how to split Anatolia between France, Greece, Italy and the UK and provide for independent areas for Armenia and Kurdistan, some Turks were taking matters into their own hands. In June 1919 the leader of the Young Turks, Mustafa Kemal Atatürk, urged his compatriots to revolt with the following stirring speech, and the 1920 Treaty of Sevres was rendered useless even before it was finalized. By 1923, the Turkish nationalists had set up a new capital in Ankara, quelled Armenian and Kurdish revolts and expelled all foreign troops, and the independent Turkish republic was established with the Treaty of Lausanne.

We must pull on our peasant shoes, we must withdraw to the mountains, we must defend the country to the last rock. If it is the will of God that we be defeated, we must set fire to all our homes, to all our property; we must lay the country in ruins and leave it an empty desert.

"HELP TO THOSE WHO HELP THEMSELVES"
Margaret Thatcher

In a wide-ranging interview conducted with a reporter from
Woman's Own magazine on 23 September, 1987 Mrs Thatcher
refuted the idea that it was the responsibility of 'society' – i.e.
government and social services – rather than individuals,
families, friends, neighbours and communities, to look after
people. She castigated those who assume that they have an
automatic entitlement to state benefits so there is no need to
work or to take any responsibility for their own lives or the
upbringing of their children. She saw government as being there
to help people to help themselves and as a support of last resort,
for those who merited it.

I think we have gone through a period when too many children
and people have been given to understand 'I have a problem, it is
the Government's job to cope with it!' or 'I have a problem, I will
go and get a grant to cope with it!' 'I am homeless, the Government
must house me!' and so they are casting their problems on society
and who is society? There is no such thing! There are individual
men and women and there are families and no government can
do anything except through people and people look to themselves
first. It is our duty to look after ourselves and then also to help
look after our neighbour and life is a reciprocal business and
people have got the entitlements too much in mind without the
obligations, because there is no such thing as an entitlement unless
someone has first met an obligation and it is, I think, one of the
tragedies in which many of the benefits we give, which were meant
to reassure people that if they were sick or ill there was a safety net
and there was help, that many of the benefits which were meant
to help people who were unfortunate – 'It is all right, we joined
together and we have these insurance schemes to look after it.'.

That was the objective, but somehow there are some people who have been manipulating the system and so some of those help and benefits that were meant to say to people: 'All right, if you cannot get a job, you shall have a basic standard of living!'. But when people come and say: 'But what is the point of working? I can get as much on the dole!'. You say: 'Look' It is not from the dole. It is your neighbour who is supplying it and if you can earn your own living then really you have a duty to do it and you will feel very much better!'.

There is also something else I should say to them: 'If that does not give you a basic standard, you know, there are ways in which we top up the standard. You can get your housing benefit.'

But it went too far. If children have a problem, it is society that is at fault. There is no such thing as society. There is living tapestry of men and women and people and the beauty of that tapestry and the quality of our lives will depend upon how much each of us is prepared to take responsibility for ourselves and each of us prepared to turn round and help by our own efforts those who are unfortunate. And the worst things we have in life, in my view, are where children who are a great privilege and a trust – they are the fundamental great trust, but they do not ask to come into the world, we bring them into the world, they are a miracle, there is nothing like the miracle of life – we have these little innocents and the worst crime in life is when those children, who would naturally have the right to look to their parents for help, for comfort, not only just for the food and shelter but for the time, for the understanding, turn round and not only is that help not forthcoming, but they get either neglect or worse than that, cruelty.

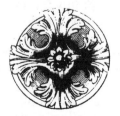

117

"DECLARING SOUTHERN RHODESIA'S INDEPENDENCE"
Ian Smith

After several years of negotiations with the British Government, which had insisted on majority rule as a condition, on 11 November, 1965 the Prime Minister of the British colony of Southern Rhodesia declared his country's independence, under white minority rule. This independence was not recognized by the international community and the United Nations imposed economic sanctions – the first time it had done so. There were several rounds of negotiations over the ensuing years, but Ian Smith continued to resist majority rule. Finally, because of the bush war and the increasing bite of sanctions, multiracial elections were held in 1979, but with a disproportionate number of parliamentary·and cabinet seats reserved for whites. The Lancaster House Agreement ended UDI and Zimbabwe gained independence in December 1979.

Whereas in the course of human affairs history has shown that it may become necessary for a people to resolve the political affiliations which have connected them with another people and to assume amongst other nations the separate and equal status to which they are entitled:

And whereas in such event a respect for the opinions of mankind requires them to declare to other nations the causes which impel them to assume full responsibility for their own affairs:

Now therefore, we, the Government of Rhodesia, do hereby declare:

That it is an indisputable and accepted historic fact that since 1923 the Government of Rhodesia have exercised the powers of self-government and have been responsible for the progress, development and welfare of their people;

That the people of Rhodesia having demonstrated their loyalty to the Crown and to their kith and kin in the United Kingdom and elsewhere through two world wars, and having been prepared to shed their blood and give of their substance in what they believed to be the mutual interests of freedom-loving people, now see all that they have cherished about to be shattered on the rocks of expediency;

That the people of Rhodesia have witnessed a process which is destructive of those very precepts upon which civilization in a primitive country has been built, they have seen the principles of Western democracy, responsible government and moral standards crumble elsewhere, nevertheless they have remained steadfast;

That the people of Rhodesia fully support the requests of their government for sovereign independence but have witnessed the consistent refusal of the Government of the United Kingdom to accede to their entreaties;

That the Government of the United Kingdom have thus demonstrated that they are not prepared to grant sovereign independence to Rhodesia on terms acceptable to the people of Rhodesia, thereby persisting in maintaining an unwarrantable jurisdiction over Rhodesia, obstructing laws and treaties with other states and the conduct of affairs with other nations and refusing assent to laws necessary for the public good, all this to the detriment of the future peace, prosperity and good government of Rhodesia;

That the Government of Rhodesia have for a long period patiently and in good faith negotiated with the Government of the United Kingdom for the removal of the remaining limitations placed upon them and for the grant of sovereign independence;

That in the belief that procrastination and delay strike at and injure the very life of the nation, the Government of Rhodesia consider it essential that Rhodesia should attain, without delay, sovereign independence, the justice of which is beyond question;

Now therefore, we the Government of Rhodesia, in humble submission to Almighty God who controls the destinies of nations, conscious that the people of Rhodesia have always shown unswerving loyalty and devotion to Her Majesty the Queen and earnestly praying that we and the people of Rhodesia will not be hindered in our determination to continue exercising our undoubted right to demonstrate the same loyalty and devotion, and seeking to promote the common good so that the dignity and freedom of all men may be assured, do, by this proclamation, adopt enact and give to the people of Rhodesia the constitution annexed hereto;

God Save The Queen.

"THE EIGHTEENTH BRUMAIRE OF LOUIS NAPOLEON"
Karl Marx

Karl Marx is revered by some as the world's greatest political thinker and reviled by others as the father of its most evil political system. In mid-nineteenth century Europe, wealth was held in the hands of a relatively small number of people and the vast majority lived in grinding poverty. Marx and Engels saw capitalism as unsound and thought that in the same way that it had replaced feudalism it would inevitably itself be replaced by communism. Marx used the idea in the opening lines of his The Eighteenth Brumaire of Louis Napoleon, an article that likened the December 1851 coup d'etat of Louis Napoleon with that of his uncle, Napoleon Bonaparte, on 18 November, 1799. The opening words were: 'Hegel says somewhere that all great events and personalities in world history reappear in one fashion or another. He forgot to add: the first time as tragedy, the second as farce.' This is often summarized as follows.

History repeats itself.

"EXTRACTS FROM THE FOUNDING COVENANT"
The League of Nations

In the aftermath of World War I, the League of Nations was founded in 1919 to promote the collective security of nations through diplomacy, arbitration and arms reduction. President Wilson's 14 Points of the previous year had included a call for an international organization. Different countries had differing wishes for the League's powers. Although it did have limited success, its ability to force members to comply was undermined by its lack of any powers except economic sanctions. Many also felt that the League was weakened by the USA not joining because of Congress's refusal to sign the Treaty of Versailles. The following extracts are from the League's Founding Covenant.

Part I. The Covenant of the League of Nations
THE HIGH CONTRACTING PARTIES.

IN ORDER TO PROMOTE international co-operation and to achieve international peace and security by the acceptance of obligations not to resort to war by the prescription of open, just and honourable relations between nations by the firm establishment of the understandings of international law as the actual rule of conduct among Governments, and by the maintenance of justice and a scrupulous respect for all treaty obligations in the dealings of organised peoples with one another AGREE to this Covenant of the League of Nations.

ARTICLE 8
The Members of the League recognise that the maintenance of peace requires the reduction of national armaments to the lowest point consistent with national safety and the enforcement by common action of international obligations.

The Council, taking account of the geographical situation and circumstances of each State, shall formulate plans for such reduction for the consideration and action of the several Governments.

Such plans shall be subject to reconsideration and revision at least every ten years.

After these plans shall have been adopted by the several Governments, the limits of armaments therein fixed shall not be exceeded without the concurrence of the Council.

The Members of the League agree that the manufacture by private enterprise of munitions and implements of war is open to grave objections. The Council shall advise how the evil effects attendant upon such manufacture can be prevented, due regard being had to the necessities of those Members of the League which are not able to manufacture the munitions and implements of war necessary for their safety.

The Members of the League undertake to interchange full and frank information as to the scale of their armaments, their military, naval, and air programmes and the condition of such of their industries as are adaptable to war-like purposes.

ARTICLE 10
The Members of the League undertake to respect and preserve as against external aggression the territorial integrity and existing political independence of all Members of the League. In case of any such aggression or in case of any threat or danger of such aggression the Council shall advise upon the means by which this obligation shall be fulfilled.

ARTICLE 11
Any war or threat of war, whether immediately affecting any of the Members of the League or not, is hereby declared a matter of concern to the whole League, and the League shall take any action that may be deemed wise and effectual to safeguard the peace of nations. In case any such emergency should arise the Secretary General shall on the request of any Member of the League forthwith summon a meeting of the Council.

It is also declared to be the friendly right of each Member of the

League to bring to the attention of the Assembly or of the Council any circumstance whatever affecting international relations which threatens to disturb international peace or the good understanding between nations upon which peace depends.

ARTICLE 12

The Members of the League agree that if there should arise between them any dispute likely to lead to a rupture, they will submit the matter either to arbitration or to inquiry by the Council, and they agree in no case to resort to war until three months after the award by the arbitrators or the report by the Council.

In any case under this Article the award of the arbitrators shall be made within a reasonable time, and the report of the Council shall be made within six months after the submission of the dispute.

ARTICLE 13

The Members of the League agree that whenever any dispute shall arise between them which they recognise to be suitable for submission to arbitration and which cannot be satisfactorily settled by diplomacy, they will submit the whole subject-matter to arbitration.

Disputes as to the interpretation of a treaty, as to any question of international law, as to the existence of any fact which if established would constitute a breach of any international obligation, or as to the extent and nature of the reparation to be made or any such breach, are declared to be among those which are generally suitable for submission to arbitration.

For the consideration of any such dispute the court of arbitration to which the case is referred shall be the Court agreed on by the parties to the dispute or stipulated in any convention existing between them.

The Members of the League agree that they will carry out in full good faith any award that may be rendered, and that they will not resort to war against a Member of the League which complies therewith. In the event of any failure to carry out such an award, the Council shall propose what steps should be taken to give effect thereto.

ARTICLE 15

If there should arise between Members of the League any dispute likely to lead to a rupture, which is not submitted to arbitration in accordance with Article 13, the Members of the League agree that they will submit the matter to the Council. Any party to the dispute may effect such submission by giving notice of the existence of the dispute to the Secretary General, who will make all necessary arrangements for a full investigation and consideration thereof . . .

ARTICLE 16

Should any Member of the League resort to war in disregard of its covenants under Articles 12, 13, or 15, it shall ipso facto be deemed to have committed an act of war against all other Members of the League, which hereby undertake immediately to subject it to the severance of all trade or financial relations, the prohibition of all intercourse between their nations and the nationals of the covenant-breaking State, and the prevention of all financial, commercial, or personal intercourse between the nationals of the covenant-breaking State and the nationals of any other State, whether a Member of the League or not.

It shall be the duty of the Council in such case to recommend to the several Governments concerned what effective military, naval, or air force the Members of the League shall severally contribute to the armed forces to be used to protect the covenants of the League.

The Members of the League agree, further, that they will mutually support one another in the financial and economic measures which are taken under this Article, in order to minimise the loss and inconvenience resulting from the above measures, and that they will mutually support one another in resisting any special measures aimed at one of their number by the covenant-breaking State, and that they will take the necessary steps to afford passage through their territory to the forces of any of the Members of the League which are co-operating to protect the covenants of the League.

Any Member of the League which has violated any covenant of the League may be declared to be no longer a Member of the League by a vote of the Council concurred in by the

Representatives of all the other Members of the League represented thereon.

ARTICLE 17

In the event of a dispute between a Member of the League and a State which is not a Member of the League, or between States not Members of the League, the State or States, not Members of the League shall be invited to accept the obligations of membership in the League for the purposes of such dispute, upon such conditions as the Council may deem just. If such invitation is accepted, the provisions of Articles 12 to 16 inclusive shall be applied with such modifications as may be deemed necessary by the Council.

Upon such invitation being given the Council shall immediately institute an inquiry into the circumstances of the dispute and recommend such action as may seem best and most effectual in the circumstances.

If a State so invited shall refuse to accept the obligations of membership in the League for the purposes of such dispute, and shall resort to war against a Member of the League, the provisions of Article 16 shall be applicable as against the State taking such action.

If both parties to the dispute when so invited refuse to accept the obligations of membership in the League for the purpose of such dispute, the Council may take such measures and make such recommendations as will prevent hostilities and will result in the settlement of the dispute.

ARTICLE 18

Every treaty or international engagement entered into hereafter by any Member of the League shall be forthwith registered with the Secretariat and shall as soon as possible be published by it. No such treaty or international engagement shall be binding until so registered.

"THE ENDING OF BRITISH RULE IN INDIA IS AN URGENT NECESSITY"
The All India Congress

As a colony of the British Empire, India was brought into World War II whether its people agreed or not. Participation by people from the subcontinent was reluctant. The All-India Congress Committee had, in 1939 passed a resolution offering conditional support for the fight against fascism but asked for independence in return, which was rejected by the British. In 1942, Sir Stafford Cripps arrived in India to negotiate devolution after the war in return for immediate co-operation. He failed and on 8 August the Committee issued the 'Quit India Resolution'. The leaders were arrested and most remained incarcerated for the next three years.

The All-India Congress Committee has given the most careful consideration to the reference made to it by the Working Committee in their resolution dated July 14, 1942, and to subsequent events, including the development of the war situation, the utterances of responsible spokesmen of the British Government, and the comments and criticisms made in India and abroad. The Committee approves of and endorses that resolution, and is of opinion that events subsequent to it have given it further justification, and have made it clear that the immediate ending of British rule in India is an urgent necessity, both for the sake of India and for the success of the cause of the United Nations. The continuation of that rule is degrading and enfeebling India and making her progressively less capable of defending herself and of contributing to the cause of world freedom . . .

The ending of British rule in this country is thus a vital and immediate issue on which depend the future of the war and the success of freedom and democracy. A free India will assure this success by throwing all her great resources in the struggle for freedom and against the aggression of Nazism, Fascism and Imperialism. This will not only affect materially the fortunes of the war, but will bring all subject and oppressed humanity on the side of the United Nations and give these nations, whose ally India would be the moral and spiritual leadership of the world. India in bondage will continue to be the symbol of British Imperialism and the taint of that imperialism will affect the fortunes of all the United Nations.

The peril of today, therefore, necessitates the independence of India and the ending of British domination. No future promises or guarantees can affect the present situation or meet that peril. They cannot produce the needed psychological effect on the mind of the masses. Only the glow of freedom now can release that energy and enthusiasm of millions of people which will immediately transform the nature of the war.

The AICC therefore, repeats with all emphasis the demand for the withdrawal of the British power from India. On the declaration of India's independence, a provincial Government will be formed and free India will become an ally of the United Nations, sharing with them in the trials and tribulations of the joint enterprise of the struggle for freedom. The provincial Government can only be formed by the cooperation of the principal parties and groups in the country. It will thus be a composite Government representative of all important sections of the people of India. Its primary functions must be to defend India and resist aggression with all the armed as well as the non-violent forces at its command, together with its Allied Powers, and to promote the well-being and progress of the workers in the fields and factories and elsewhere to whom essentially all power and authority must belong. The provincial Government will evolve a scheme for a constituent assembly which will prepare a constitution for the Government of India acceptable to all sections of the people. This constitution according to the Congress view, should be a federal one. With the largest measure of autonomy for the federating units, and with the residuary powers vesting in these units. The future relations between India and the Allied Nations will be adjusted by representatives of all these free countries conferring together for their mutual advantage and for their co-operation in the common task of resisting aggression. Freedom will enable India to resist aggression effectively with the people's united will and strength behind it.

The freedom of India must be the symbol of and prelude to this freedom of all other Asiatic nations under foreign domination. Burma, Malaya, Indo-China, the Dutch Indies, Iran and Iraq must also attain their complete freedom. It must be clearly understood that such of these countries as are under Japanese control now must not subsequently be placed under the rule or control of any other Colonial Power.

While the AICC must primarily be concerned with the independence and defence of India in this hour of danger, the Committee is of opinion that the future peace, security and ordered progress of the world demand a world federation of free nations, and on no other basis can the problems of the modern world be solved. Such a world federation would ensure the freedom of its constituent nations, the prevention of aggression and exploitation by one nation over another the protection of national minorities, the advancement of all backward areas and peoples, and the pooling of the world's resources for the common good of all. On the establishment of such a world federation, disarmament would be practicable in all countries, national armies, navies and air forces would no longer be necessary, and a world federal defence force would keep the world peace and prevent aggression.

An independent India would gladly join such a world federation and co-operate on an equal basis with other countries in the solution of international problems. Such a federation should be open to all nations who agree with its fundamental principles. In view of the war, however, the federation must inevitably, to begin with, be confined to the United Nations, such a step taken now will have a most powerful effect on the war, on the peoples of the Axis countries, and on the peace to come.

The Committee regretfully realizes, however, despite the tragic and overwhelming lessons of the war and the perils that overhang the world, the Governments of few countries are yet prepared to take this inevitable step towards world federation. The reactions of the British Government and the misguided criticism of the foreign Press also make it clear that even the obvious demand for India's independence is resisted, though this has been made essentially to meet the present peril and to enable India to defend herself and help China and Russia in their hour of need. The Committee is anxious not to embarrass in any way the defence of China or Russia, whose freedom is precious and must be preserved, or to jeopardise the defensive capacity of the United Nations. But the peril grows both to India and these nations, and inaction and submission to a foreign administration at this stage is not only degrading India and reducing her capacity to defend herself and resist aggression but is no answer to that knowing peril and is no service to the peoples of the United Nations. The earnest appeal of the Working Committee to Great Britain and the United Nations has so far met with no response and the criticism made in many foreign quarters have shown an ignorance of India's and the world's need, and sometimes even hostility to India's freedom, which is significant of a mentality of domination and racial superiority which cannot be tolerated by a proud people conscious of their strength and of the justice of their cause.

"POLITICS WITHOUT PRINCIPLES"
Mohandas K. Gandhi

After spending two years of a six-year sentence in prison for sedition between 1922 and 1924, Indian independence campaigner Gandhi steered clear of active politics for a few years, concentrating instead on social and human rights issues, such as those of the untouchables. His seven social sins list is a blueprint for what he perceived was wrong with life in India at the time. It was first published in written form in *Young India*, the English-language magazine that he published in order to gain a wider audience for his spoken teachings and philosophy. Each of the sins suggests an ideal opposite based on permanent natural principles rather than transient social or cultural values, such as politics with principles and science with humanity.

Politics without principles
Wealth without work
Pleasure without conscience
Knowledge without character
Commerce without morality
Science without humanity
Worship without sacrifice

"BARACK OBAMA'S INAUGURAL ADDRESS"
Barack Obama

In comparison to the upbeat nature of his acceptance speech on 4 November, 2008, President Obama's Inaugural Address was a sober call to restore responsibility – both political and personal – and a pledge to bring about change while respecting the traditions and values of the American people. On a freezing Washington day, standing behind a bullet-proof shield and looking out over the estimated 1,800,000 people on the National Mall stretching towards the Washington Monument, the new President spoke the following words:

My fellow citizens: I stand here today humbled by the task before us, grateful for the trust you have bestowed, mindful of the sacrifices borne by our ancestors. I thank President Bush for his service to our nation, as well as the generosity and co-operation he has shown throughout this transition.

The words have been spoken during rising tides of prosperity and the still waters of peace. Yet, every so often the oath is taken amidst gathering clouds and raging storms. At these moments, America has carried on not simply because of the skill or vision of those in high office, but because We the People have remained faithful to the ideals of our forbearers, and true to our founding documents.

So it has been. So it must be with this generation of Americans.

That we are in the midst of crisis is now well understood. Our nation is at war, against a far-reaching network of violence and hatred. Our economy is badly weakened, a consequence of greed and irresponsibility on the part of some, but also our collective failure to make hard choices and prepare the nation for a new age. Homes have been lost; jobs shed; businesses shuttered. Our health care is too costly; our schools fail too many; and each day brings further evidence that the ways we use energy strengthen our adversaries and threaten our planet.

These are the indicators of crisis, subject to data and statistics. Less measurable but no less profound is a sapping of confidence across our land – a nagging fear that America's decline is inevitable, and that the next generation must lower its sights.

Today I say to you that the challenges we face are real. They are serious and they are many. They will not be met easily or in a short span of time. But know this, America – they will be met.

On this day, we gather because we have chosen hope over fear, unity of purpose over conflict and discord.

On this day, we come to proclaim an end to the petty grievances and false promises, the recriminations and worn out dogmas, that for far too long have strangled our politics.

We remain a young nation, but in the words of Scripture, the time has come to set aside childish things. The time has come to reaffirm our enduring spirit; to choose our better history; to carry forward that precious gift, that noble idea, passed on from generation to generation: the God-given promise that all are equal, all are free, and all deserve a chance to pursue their full measure of happiness.

In reaffirming the greatness of our nation, we understand that greatness is never a given. It must be earned. Our journey has never been one of short-cuts or settling for less. It has not been the path for the faint-hearted – for those who prefer leisure over work, or seek only the pleasures of riches and fame.

Rather, it has been the risk-takers, the doers, the makers of things – some celebrated but more often men and women obscure in their labour, who have carried us up the long, rugged path towards prosperity and freedom.

For us, they packed up their few worldly possessions and travelled across oceans in search of a new life.

For us, they toiled in sweatshops and settled the West; endured the lash of the whip and ploughed the hard earth.

For us, they fought and died, in places like Concord and Gettysburg; Normandy and Khe Sahn.

Time and again these men and women struggled and sacrificed and worked till their hands were raw so that we might live a better life. They saw America as bigger than the sum of our individual ambitions; greater than all the differences of birth or wealth or faction.

This is the journey we continue today. We remain the most prosperous, powerful nation on Earth. Our workers are no less productive than when this crisis began.

Our minds are no less inventive, our goods and services no less needed than they were last week or last month or last year. Our capacity remains undiminished.

But our time of standing pat, of protecting narrow interests and putting off unpleasant decisions – that time has surely passed. Starting today, we must pick ourselves up, dust ourselves off, and begin again the work of remaking America.

For everywhere we look, there is work to be done. The state of the economy calls for action, bold and swift, and we will act – not only to create new jobs, but to lay a new foundation for growth. We will build the roads and bridges, the electric grids and digital lines that feed our commerce and bind us together. We will restore science to its rightful place, and wield technology's wonders to raise health care's quality and lower its cost. We will harness the sun and the winds and the soil to fuel our cars and run our factories. And we will transform our schools and colleges and universities to meet the demands of a new age. All this we can do. And all this we will do.

Now, there are some who question the scale of our ambitions – who suggest that our system cannot tolerate too many big plans.

Their memories are short. For they have forgotten what this country has already done; what free men and women can achieve when imagination is joined to common purpose, and necessity to courage.

What the cynics fail to understand is that the ground has shifted beneath them – that the stale political arguments that have consumed us for so long no longer apply. The question we ask today is not whether our government is too big or too small, but whether it works – whether it helps families find jobs at a decent wage, care they can afford, a retirement that is dignified. Where the answer is yes, we intend to move forward. Where the answer is no, programs will end. And those of us who manage the public's dollars will be held to account – to spend wisely, reform bad habits, and do our business in the light of day – because only then can we restore the vital trust between a people and their government.

Nor is the question before us whether the market is a force for good or ill.

Its power to generate wealth and expand freedom is unmatched, but this crisis has reminded us that without a watchful eye, the market can spin out of control – and that a nation cannot prosper long when it favours only the prosperous. The success of our economy has always depended not just on the size of our gross domestic product, but on the reach of our prosperity; on our ability to extend opportunity to every willing heart – not out of charity, but because it is the surest route to our common good. As for our common defence, we reject as false the choice between our safety and our ideals. Our Founding Fathers, faced with perils we can scarcely imagine, drafted a charter to assure the rule of law and the rights of man, a charter expanded by the blood of generations. Those ideals still light the world, and we will not give them up for expedience's sake. And so to all other peoples and governments who are watching today, from the grandest capitals to the small village where my father was born: know that America is a friend of each nation and every man, woman, and child who seeks a future of peace and dignity, and that we are ready to lead once more. Recall that earlier generations faced down fascism and communism not just with missiles and tanks, but with sturdy alliances and enduring convictions. They understood that our power alone cannot protect us, nor does it entitle us to do as we please. Instead, they knew that our power grows through its prudent use; our security emanates from the justness of our cause, the force of our example, the tempering qualities of humility and restraint. We are the keepers of this legacy. Guided by these principles once more, we can meet those new threats that demand even greater effort – even greater cooperation and understanding between nations. We will begin to responsibly leave Iraq to its people, and forge a hard-earned peace in Afghanistan. With old friends and former foes, we will work tirelessly to lessen the nuclear threat, and roll back the spectre of a warming planet. We will not apologise for our way of life, nor will we waver in its defense, and for those who seek to advance their aims by inducing terror and slaughtering innocents, we say to you now that our spirit is stronger and cannot be broken; you cannot outlast us, and we will defeat you. For we know that our patchwork heritage is a strength, not a weakness. We are a nation of Christians and Muslims, Jews and Hindus – and non-believers. We are shaped by every language and culture, drawn from every end of this Earth; and because we have tasted the bitter swill of civil war and segregation, and emerged from that dark chapter stronger and more united, we cannot help but believe that the old hatreds shall someday pass; that the lines of tribe shall soon dissolve; that as the world grows smaller, our common humanity shall reveal itself; and that America must play its role in ushering in a new era of peace. To the Muslim world, we seek a new way forward, based on mutual interest and mutual respect. To those leaders around the globe who seek to sow conflict, or blame their society's ills on the West – know that your people will judge you on what you can build, not what you destroy. To those who cling to power through corruption and deceit and the silencing of dissent, know that you are on the wrong side of history; but that we will extend a hand if you are willing to unclench your fist. To the people of poor nations, we pledge to work alongside you to make your farms flourish and let clean waters flow; to nourish starved bodies and feed hungry minds. And to those nations like ours that enjoy relative plenty, we say we can no longer afford indifference to suffering outside our borders; nor can we consume the world's resources without regard to effect. For the world has changed, and we must change with it. As we consider the road that unfolds before us, we remember with humble gratitude those brave Americans who, at this very hour, patrol far-off deserts and distant mountains. They have something to tell us today, just as the fallen heroes who lie in Arlington whisper through the ages. We honor them not only because they are guardians of our liberty, but because they embody the spirit of service; a willingness to find meaning in something greater than themselves. And yet, at this moment – a moment that will define a generation – it is precisely this spirit that must inhabit us all. For as much as government can do and must do, it is ultimately the faith and determination of the American people upon which this nation relies. It is the kindness to take in a stranger when the levees break, the selflessness of workers who would rather cut their hours than see a friend lose their job which sees us through our darkest hours. It is the fire-fighter's courage to storm a stairway filled with smoke, but also a parent's willingness to nurture a child, that finally decides our fate. Our challenges may be new. The instruments with which we meet them may be new. But those values upon which our success depends – hard work and honesty, courage and fair play, tolerance and curiosity, loyalty and patriotism – these things are old. These things are true. They have been the quiet force of progress throughout our history. What is demanded then is a return to these truths. What is required of us now is a new era of responsibility – a recognition, on the part of every American, that we have duties to ourselves, our nation, and the world, duties that we do not grudgingly accept but rather seize gladly, firm in the knowledge that there is nothing so satisfying to the spirit, so defining of our character, than giving our all to a difficult task. This is the price and the promise of citizenship. This is the source of our confidence – the knowledge that God calls on us to shape an uncertain destiny. This is the meaning of our liberty and our creed – why men and women and children of every race and every faith can join in celebration across this magnificent mall, and why a man whose father less than 60 years ago might not have been served at a local restaurant can now stand before you to take a most sacred oath. So let us mark this day with remembrance, of who we are and how far we have travelled. In the year of America's birth, in the coldest of months, a small band of patriots huddled by dying campfires on the shores of an icy river. The capital was abandoned. The enemy was advancing. The snow was stained with blood. At a moment when the outcome of our revolution was most in doubt, the father of our nation ordered these words be read to the people: 'Let it be told to the future world . . . that in the depth of winter, when nothing but hope and virtue could survive . . . that the city and the country, alarmed at one common danger, came forth to meet [it].' America. In the face of our common dangers, in this winter of our hardship, let us remember these timeless words. With hope and virtue, let us brave once more the icy currents, and endure what storms may come. Let it be said by our children's children that when we were tested we refused to let this journey end, that we did not turn back nor did we falter; and with eyes fixed on the horizon and God's grace upon us, we carried forth that great gift of freedom and delivered it safely to future generations. Thank you. God bless you, and God bless the United States of America.

WAR

"HOPE THAT WAR MAY BE PREVENTED"
Neville Chamberlain

In a radio broadcast on 27 September, 1938, at the height of the crisis surrounding Germany's intention to annexe the Sudetenland, British Prime Minister Neville Chamberlain gave an update on negotiations. While he sympathized with the Czech government's attitude to the idea of giving up their defensive border, he was going to sacrifice that country's sovereignty to appease Hitler and (as he still hoped) prevent a wider war. It was a useless hope as Hitler intended to occupy the Sudetenland in any case, and for every concession Chamberlain wrenched out of the Czech government, Hitler imposed new ones.

Tomorrow Parliament is going to meet, and I shall be making a full statement of the events which have led up to the present anxious and critical situation.

An earlier statement would not have been possible when I was flying backwards and forwards across Europe, and the position was changing from hour to hour. But today there is a lull for a brief time, and I want to say a few words to you, men and women of Britain and the Empire, and perhaps to others as well.

First of all I must say something to those who have written to my wife or myself in these last weeks to tell us of their gratitude for my efforts and to assure us of their prayers for my success. Most of these letters have come from women – mothers or sisters of our own countrymen. But there are countless others besides – from France, from Belgium, from Italy, and even from Germany, and it has been heartbreaking to read the growing anxiety they reveal and their intense relief when they thought, too soon, that the danger of war was past.

If I felt my responsibility heavy before, to read such letters has made it seem almost overwhelming. How horrible, fantastic, incredible it is that we should be digging trenches and trying on gas-masks here because of a quarrel in a far-away country between people of whom we know nothing. It seems still more impossible that a quarrel which has already been settled in principle should be the subject of war.

I can well understand the reasons why the Czech Government have felt unable to accept the terms which have been put before them in the German memorandum. Yet I believe after my talks with Herr Hitler that, if only time were allowed, it ought to be possible for the arrangements for transferring the territory that the Czech Government has agreed to give to Germany to be settled by agreement under conditions which would assure fair treatment to the population concerned.

You know already that I have done all that one man can do to compose this quarrel. After my visits to Germany I have realised vividly how Herr Hitler feels that he must champion other Germans, and his indignation that grievances have not been met before this. He told me privately, and last night he repeated publicly, that after this Sudeten German question is settled, that is the end of Germany's territorial claims in Europe.

After my first visit to Berchtesgaden I did get the assent of the Czech Government to proposals which gave the substance of what Herr Hitler wanted and I was taken completely by surprise when I got back to Germany and found that he insisted that the territory should be handed over to him immediately, and immediately occupied by German troops without previous arrangements for safeguarding the people within the territory who were not Germans, or did not want to join the German Reich.

I must say that I find this attitude unreasonable. If it arises out of any doubts that Herr Hitler feels about the intentions of the Czech Government to carry out their promises and hand over the territory, I have offered on part of the British Government to guarantee their words, and I am sure the value of our promise will not be underrated anywhere.

I shall not give up the hope of a peaceful solution, or abandon my efforts for peace, as long as any chance for peace remains. I would not hesitate to pay even a third visit to Germany if I thought it would do any good. But at this moment I see nothing further that I can usefully do in the way of mediation.

Meanwhile there are certain things we can and shall do at home. Volunteers are still wanted for air raid precautions, for fire brigade and police services, and for the Territorial units. I know that all of you, men and women alike, are ready to play your part in the defence of the country, and I ask you all to offer your services, if you have not already done so, to the local authorities, who will tell you if you are wanted and in what capacity.

Do not be alarmed if you hear of men being called up to man the anti-aircraft defences or ships. These are only precautionary measures such as a Government must take in times like this. But they do not necessarily mean that we have determined on war or that war is imminent.

However much we may sympathise with a small nation confronted by a big and powerful neighbour, we cannot in all circumstances undertake to involve the whole British Empire in war simply on her account. If we have to fight it must be on larger issues than that. I am myself a man of peace to the depths of my soul. Armed conflict between nations is a nightmare to me; but if I were convinced that any nation had made up its mind to dominate the world by fear of its force, I should feel that it must be resisted. Under such a domination life for people who believe in liberty would not be worth living; but war is a fearful thing, and we must be very clear, before we embark on it, that it is really the great issues that are at stake, and that the call to risk everything in their defence, when all the consequences are weighed, is irresistible.

For the present I ask you to wait as calmly as you can the events of the next few days. As long as war has not begun, there is always hope that it may be prevented, and you know that I am going to work for peace to the last moment. Good night.

"DURING THE VIOLENT REVOLT IN IRELAND"
Oliver Cromwell

After the deposition and death of Charles I in January 1649, the Irish Catholic population and the Scots began violent revolts against British rule and murdered large numbers of Protestants. Cromwell led an army to Ireland to defeat the rebellion, but the cruelty of his actions in suppressing it, by which the populations of entire towns were slaughtered, led to centuries of resentment. Because it was a Catholic rebellion he appears to have seen it in terms of a holy war. The following year, he undertook a similar operation against the rebelling Scots who had proclaimed the son of the old King, monarch. Because they were predominantly Presbyterians, he was less blood-thirsty than in Ireland.

Put your trust in God, my boys, and keep your powder dry.

"FOR THE FALLEN"
Laurence Binyon

This poem was written by Laurence Binyon at the outbreak of
World War I when the toll of casualties was a shock to everyone.
It is widely used at Remembrance Day services in many
Commonwealth countries and at Anzac Day commemorations
in Australia and New Zealand. The last line of the fourth verse
– the citation – is repeated. Binyon worked in the British
Museum in London and was too old to be drafted for active
service, but volunteered for work as a medical orderly with an
ambulance unit on the Western Front in 1916. He is
commemorated on a slab in Westminster Abbey's Poets Corner,
along with other war poets such as Wilfred Owen.

FOR THE FALLEN

With proud thanksgiving, a mother for her children,
England mourns for her dead across the sea.
Flesh of her flesh they were, spirit of her spirit,
Fallen in the cause of the free.

Solemn the drums thrill; Death august and royal
Sings sorrow up into immortal spheres,
There is music in the midst of desolation
And a glory that shines upon our tears.

They went with songs to the battle, they were young,
Straight of limb, true of eye, steady and aglow.
They were staunch to the end against odds uncounted;
They fell with their faces to the foe.

They shall grow not old, as we that are left grow old:
Age shall not weary them, nor the years condemn.

At the going down of the Sun and in the morning
We will remember them. We will remember them.

They mingle not with their laughing comrades again;
They sit no more at familiar tables of home;
They have no lot in our labour of the day-time;
They sleep beyond England's foam.

But where our desires are and our hopes profound,
Felt as a well-spring that is hidden from sight,
To the innermost heart of their own land they are known
As the stars are known to the Night.

As the stars that shall be bright when we are dust,
Moving in marches upon the heavenly plain;
As the stars that are starry in the time of our darkness,
To the end, to the end, they remain

"CHANCE FOR PEACE"
Dwight D. Eisenhower

In one of his first major speeches after his inauguration – known as the 'chance for peace' speech – President Eisenhower spoke to the American Society of Newspaper Editors on 16 April, 1953. As Supreme Allied Commander in Europe during World War II and a veteran of World War I, he had seen enough war to last a lifetime and pledged to use the nation's wealth for better projects. Within weeks he had signed the armistice that ended the Korean War and by the end of the year he had outlined his proposals for a body concerned with nuclear cooperation and monitoring, which was set up in 1957 as the 'Atoms for Peace' organization – now the International Atomic Energy Agency.

. . . In this spring of 1953 the free world weighs one question above all others: the chances for a just peace for all peoples. To weigh this chance is to summon instantly to mind another recent moment of great decision. It came with that yet more hopeful spring of 1945, bright with the promise of victory and of freedom. The hopes of all just men in that moment, too, was a just and lasting peace . . .

This common purpose lasted an instant and perished. The nations of the world divided to follow two distinct roads . . .

The way chosen by the United States was plainly marked by a few clear precepts, which govern its conduct in world affairs . . .

This way was faithful to the spirit that inspired the United Nations: to prohibit strife, to relieve tensions, to banish fears. This way was to control and to reduce armaments. This way was to allow all nations to devote their energies and resources to the great and good tasks of healing the war's wounds, of clothing and feeding and housing the needy, of perfecting a just political life, of enjoying the fruits of their own toil.

The Soviet government held a vastly different vision of the

future. In the world of its design, security was to be found, not in mutual trust and mutual aid but in force: huge armies, subversion, rule of neighbor nations. The goal was power superiority at all cost. Security was to be sought by denying it to all others . . .

The amassing of Soviet power alerted free nations to a new danger of aggression. It compelled them in self-defense to spend unprecedented money and energy for armaments. It forced them to develop weapons of war now capable of inflicting instant and terrible punishment upon any aggressor.

It instilled in the free nations . . . the unshakable conviction that, as long as there persists a threat to freedom, they must, at any cost, remain armed, strong, and ready for the risk of war.

It inspired them – and let none doubt this – to attain a unity of purpose and will beyond the power of propaganda or pressure to break, now or ever . . .

The free nations, most solemnly and repeatedly, have assured the Soviet Union that their firm association has never had any aggressive purpose whatsoever. Soviet leaders, however, have seemed to persuade themselves, or tried to persuade their people, otherwise.

And so it has come to pass that the Soviet Union itself has shared and suffered the very fears it has fostered in the rest of the world . . .

What can the world, or any nation in it, hope for if no turning is found on this dread road?

The worst to be feared and the best to be expected can be simply stated.

The worst is atomic war.

The best would be this: a life of perpetual fear and tension; a burden of arms draining the wealth and the labor of all peoples; a wasting of strength that defies the American system or the Soviet system or any system to achieve true abundance and happiness for the peoples of this Earth . . .

This is one of those times in the affairs of nations when the gravest choices must be made, if there is to be a turning toward a just and lasting peace.

It is a moment that calls upon the governments of the world to speak their intentions with simplicity and with honesty.

It calls upon them to answer the question that stirs the hearts of all sane men: is there no other way the world may live? . . .

The free world knows, out of the bitter wisdom of experience, that vigilance and sacrifice are the price of liberty . . .

So the new Soviet leadership now has a precious opportunity to awaken, with the rest of the world, to the point of peril reached and to help turn the tide of history.

Will it do this?

We do not yet know. Recent statements and gestures of Soviet leaders give some evidence that they may recognize this critical moment . . .

As progress in all these areas strengthens world trust, we could proceed concurrently with the next great work – the reduction of the burden of armaments now weighing upon the world. To this end we would welcome and enter into the most solemn agreements . . .

The peace we seek, founded upon decent trust and cooperative effort among nations, can be fortified, not by weapons of war but by wheat and by cotton, by milk and by wool, by meat and timber and rice. These are words that translate into every language on Earth. These are the needs that challenge this world in arms . . .

We are prepared to reaffirm, with the most concrete evidence, our readiness to help build a world in which all peoples can be productive and prosperous . . .

I know of only one question upon which progress waits. It is this: What is the Soviet Union ready to do? . . .

. . . where then is the concrete evidence of the Soviet Union's concern for peace?

There is, before all peoples, a precarious chance to turn the black tide of events.

If we fail to strive to seize this chance, the judgment of future ages will be harsh and just.

If we strive but fail and the world remains armed against itself, it at least would need be divided no longer in its clear knowledge of who has condemned humankind to this fate.

The purpose of the United States, in stating these proposals, is simple. These proposals spring, without ulterior motive or political passion, from our calm conviction that the hunger for peace is in the hearts of all people – those of Russia and of China no less than of our own country.

They conform to our firm faith that God created man to enjoy, not destroy, the fruits of the Earth and of their own toil.

They aspire to this: the lifting, from the backs and from the hearts of men, of their burden of arms and of fears, so that they may find before them a golden age of freedom and of peace.

"TERMINATION OF HIS ORDER OF THE DAY"
Robert Nivelle

In the early stages of World War I, Colonel Robert Nivelle had been so successful in artillery action against the Germans that he was promoted to general and was designated to lead the French Second Army at the Battle of Verdun. His tactics were successful, but costly in terms of his own soldiers' lives. The phrase quoted is the termination of his order of the day for 23 June, 1916. Over the ensuing months the French did re-take some ground, and in December he was made commander-in-chief of the French armies. Although a brilliant tactician at a local level, his inflexibility and arrogance did not make him suited to command the whole army. After the Nivelle Offensive of 1917, which cost the lives of 187,000 of his soldiers, he was removed from his command and subsequently sent to Africa.

Ils ne passeront pas! (They shall not pass!)

"THE WAR IN INDOCHINA"
Ho Chi Minh

During World War II, Vietnam had been occupied by the
Japanese and after their defeat the Viet Minh – together with
other revolutionary and nationalist groups such as the
Constitutional Party and the Party for Independence – were
determined not to allow the former colonial power, France, to
reassert control. After the August Revolution of 1945, Emperor
Bao Dai abdicated, Ho Chi Minh declared independence and
the Viet Minh emerged from the ensuing bloodbath as the most
powerful party. The statement below indicates the guerrilla
tactics that his forces would use over the next eight years against
the French and again against the American army between 1965
and 1975.

If the tiger ever stands still, the elephant will crush him with his
mighty tusks. But the tiger will not stand still. He will leap upon
the back of the elephant, tearing huge chunks from his side, and
then he will leap back into the dark jungle. And slowly the elephant
will bleed to death. Such will be the war in Indochina.

"THE ABSENCE OF EVIDENCE IS NOT EVIDENCE OF ABSENCE"
Donald Rumsfeld

In a Q&A session at a NATO summit in June 2002, a journalist posed a question about terrorism and weapons of mass destruction (WMD) and what Secretary Rumsfeld meant when he said the situation was worse than generally understood. The reply hints that the intelligence community were digging into old data for clues as to whether Iraq retained – or was working on – WMD capability. This hunt resulted in such documents as the September dossier – the UK government list of (false) claims about such things as Iraqi attempts to buy uranium from Niger.

Sure. All of us in this business read intelligence information. And we read it daily and we think about it and it becomes, in our minds, essentially what exists. And that's wrong. It is not what exists.

I say that because I have had experiences where I have gone back and done a great deal of work and analysis on intelligence information and looked at important countries, target countries, looked at important subject matters with respect to those target countries and asked, probed deeper and deeper and kept probing until I found out what it is we knew, and when we learned it, and when it actually had existed. And I found that, not to my surprise, but I think anytime you look at it that way what you find is that there are very important pieces of intelligence information that countries, that spend a lot of money, and a lot of time with a lot of wonderful people trying to learn more about what's going in the world, did not know some significant event for two years after it happened, for four years after it happened, for six years after it happened, in some cases 11 and 12 and 13 years after it happened.

Now what is the message there? The message is that there are no 'knowns'. There are things we know that we know. There are known unknowns. That is to say there are things that we now know we don't know. But there are also unknown unknowns. There are things we don't know we don't know. So when we do the best we can and we pull all this information together, and we then say well that's basically what we see as the situation, that is really only the known knowns and the known unknowns. And each year, we discover a few more of those unknown unknowns.

It sounds like a riddle. It isn't a riddle. It is a very serious, important matter.

There's another way to phrase that and that is that the absence of evidence is not evidence of absence. It is basically saying the same thing in a different way. Simply because you do not have evidence that something exists does not mean that you have evidence that it doesn't exist. And yet almost always, when we make our threat assessments, when we look at the world, we end up basing it on the first two pieces of that puzzle, rather than all three.

"PEACE WITHOUT VICTORY"
Woodrow Wilson

On 22 January, 1917 President Wilson addressed the Senate saying that he had had communications with representatives from both sides in Europe. He outlined the need for 'peace without victory' where no party would feel overly aggrieved, all countries would be equal in rights and people would not be forced to swap from one power to another. The ideas in this speech would emerge in a more concrete form in the 'Fourteen Points of Peace' speech the following year. The idea of not inflicting a humiliating defeat on Germany did not appeal to the French, and the subsequent punitive reparations and restrictions on armaments that were imposed caused resentment among Germans and the growth of groups such as the Nazis.

On the eighteenth of December last I addressed an identic note to the governments of the nations now at war requesting them to state, more definitely than they had yet been stated by either group of belligerents, the terms upon which they would deem it possible to make peace. I spoke on behalf of humanity and of the rights of all neutral nations like our own, many of whose most vital interests the war puts in constant jeopardy. The Central Powers united in a reply which stated merely that they were ready to meet their antagonists in conference to discuss terms of peace. The Entente Powers have replied much more definitely and have stated, in general terms, indeed, but with sufficient definiteness to imply details, the arrangements, guarantees, and acts of reparation which they deem to be the indispensable conditions of a satisfactory settlement. We are that much nearer a definite discussion of the peace which shall end the present war. We are that much nearer the discussion of the international concert which must thereafter hold the world at peace. In every discussion of the peace that must end this war it is taken for granted that that peace must be followed by some definite concert of power which will make it virtually impossible that any such catastrophe should ever overwhelm us again. Every lover of mankind, every sane and thoughtful man must take that for granted.

I have sought this opportunity to address you because I thought that I owed it to you, as the council associated with me in the final determination of our international obligations, to disclose to you without reserve the thought and purpose that have been taking form in my mind in regard to the duty of our Government in the days to come when it will be necessary to lay afresh and upon a new plan the foundations of peace among the nations.

It is inconceivable that the people of the United States should play no part in that great enterprise. To take part in such a service will be the opportunity for which they have sought to prepare themselves by the very principles and purposes of their polity and the approved practices of their Government ever since the days when they set up a new nation in the high and honourable hope that it might in all that it was and did show mankind the way to liberty. They cannot in honour withhold the service to which they are now about to be challenged. They do not wish to withhold it. But they owe it to themselves and to the other nations of the world to state the conditions under which they will feel free to render it.

That service is nothing less than this, to add their authority and their power to the authority and force of other nations to guarantee peace and justice throughout the world. Such a settlement cannot now be long postponed. It is right that before it comes this Government should frankly formulate the conditions upon which it would feel justified in asking our people to approve its formal and solemn adherence to a League for Peace. I am here to attempt to state those conditions.

The present war must first be ended; but we owe it to candour and to a just regard for the opinion of mankind to say that, so far as our participation in guarantees of future peace is concerned, it makes a great deal of difference in what way and upon what terms it is ended. The treaties and agreements which bring it to an end must embody terms which will create a peace that is worth guaranteeing and preserving, a peace that will win the approval of mankind, not merely a peace that will serve the several interests

155

and immediate aims of the nations engaged. We shall have no voice in determining what those terms shall be, but we shall, I feel sure, have a voice in determining whether they shall be made lasting or not by the guarantees of a universal covenant; and our judgment upon what is fundamental and essential as a condition precedent to permanency should be spoken now, not afterwards when it may be too late.

No covenant of cooperative peace that does not include the peoples of the New World can suffice to keep the future safe against war; and yet there is only one sort of peace that the peoples of America could join in guaranteeing. The elements of that peace must be elements that engage the confidence and satisfy the principles of the American governments, elements consistent with their political faith and with the practical convictions which the peoples of America have once for all embraced and undertaken to defend . . .

"IF THE IRAQI REGIME WISHES PEACE . . ."
George W. Bush

The day after the anniversary of 9/11, President Bush addressed the UN General Assembly about his government's intentions with regard to Iraq. He detailed the 16 UN resolutions concerned with illegal weapons, sanctions-busting, prisoners of war and human rights issues that he claimed Saddam was breaking and getting away with because of UN appeasement. He also stated his belief that Iraq had weapons of mass destruction and that it posed a risk to American allies in the region. The message that the US would take action, with UN backing or not, angered many.

Mr Secretary General, Mr. President, distinguished delegates, and ladies and gentlemen: We meet one year and one day after a terrorist attack brought grief to my country, and brought grief to many citizens of our world. Yesterday, we remembered the innocent lives taken that terrible morning. Today, we turn to the urgent duty of protecting other lives, without illusion and without fear . . .

Above all, our principles and our security are challenged today by outlaw groups and regimes that accept no law of morality and have no limit to their violent ambitions. In the attacks on America a year ago, we saw the destructive intentions of our enemies. This threat hides within many nations, including my own . . . And our greatest fear is that terrorists will find a shortcut to their mad ambitions when an outlaw regime supplies them with the technologies to kill on a massive scale.

In one place – in one regime – we find all these dangers, in their most lethal and aggressive forms, exactly the kind of aggressive threat the United Nations was born to confront.

Twelve years ago, Iraq invaded Kuwait without provocation. And the regime's forces were poised to continue their march to seize other countries and their resources. Had Saddam Hussein been appeased instead of stopped, he would have endangered the peace and stability of the world. Yet this aggression was stopped – by the might of coalition forces and the will of the United Nations.

To suspend hostilities, to spare himself, Iraq's dictator accepted a series of commitments. The terms were clear, to him and to all. And he agreed to prove he is complying with every one of those obligations.

He has proven instead only his contempt for the United Nations, and for all his pledges. By breaking every pledge – by his deceptions, and by his cruelties – Saddam Hussein has made the case against himself . . .

If the Iraqi regime wishes peace, it will immediately and unconditionally forswear, disclose, and remove or destroy all weapons of mass destruction, long-range missiles, and all related material.

If the Iraqi regime wishes peace, it will immediately end all support for terrorism and act to suppress it, as all states are required to do by UN Security Council resolutions.

If the Iraqi regime wishes peace, it will cease persecution of its civilian population, including Shi'a, Sunnis, Kurds, Turkomans, and others, again as required by Security Council resolutions.

If the Iraqi regime wishes peace, it will release or account for all Gulf War personnel whose fate is still unknown. It will return the remains of any who are deceased, return stolen property, accept liability for losses resulting from the invasion of Kuwait, and fully cooperate with international efforts to resolve these issues, as required by Security Council resolutions.

If the Iraqi regime wishes peace, it will immediately end all illicit trade outside the oil-for-food program. It will accept UN administration of funds from that program, to ensure that the money is used fairly and promptly for the benefit of the Iraqi people. If all these steps are taken, it will signal a new openness and accountability in Iraq. And it could open the prospect of the United Nations helping to build a government that represents all Iraqis – a government based on respect for human rights, economic liberty, and internationally supervised elections . . .

My nation will work with the UN Security Council to meet our common challenge. If Iraq's regime defies us again, the world must move deliberately, decisively to hold Iraq to account. We will work with the UN Security Council for the necessary resolutions. But the purposes of the United States should not be doubted. The Security Council resolutions will be enforced – the just demands of peace and security will be met – or action will be unavoidable. And a regime that has lost its legitimacy will also lose its power . . .

Neither of these outcomes is certain. Both have been set before us. We must choose between a world of fear and a world of progress. We cannot stand by and do nothing while dangers gather. We must stand up for our security, and for the permanent rights and the hopes of mankind. By heritage and by choice, the United States of America will make that stand. And, delegates to the United Nations, you have the power to make that stand, as well.

"SHAKING OFF THE SHACKLES OF THE VERSAILLES DICTATE"
Adolf Hitler

In May and June 1940, Hitler invaded and successively conquered Belgium, the Netherlands and northern France, with Paris falling on 14 June. A puppet government was installed in Vichy in the south. On 19 July, 1940 Hitler gave a speech at the Reichstag in which he appeared to offer peace to the UK, although the Luftwaffe had already started bombing airfields to destroy the Royal Air Force and make the projected invasion easier. This peace proposal was rejected, so Hitler ordered the air-drop of copies of the speech on the night of 1–2 August to persuade the British people not to support their government's stance.

I have summoned you to this meeting in the midst of our tremendous struggle for the freedom and the future of the German nation. I have done so, firstly, because I considered it imperative to give our people an insight into the events, unique in history, that lie behind us, secondly, because I wished to express my gratitude to our magnificent soldiers, and thirdly, with the intention of appealing, once more and for the last time, to common sense in general . . .

If we compare the causes which prompted this historic struggle with the magnitude and the far-reaching effects of military events, we are forced to the conclusion that its general course and the sacrifices it has entailed are out of proportion to the alleged reasons for its outbreak – unless they were nothing but a pretext for underlying intentions . . .

This revision [of the Treaty of Versailles] was absolutely essential. The conditions imposed at Versailles were intolerable, not only because of their humiliating discrimination and because the disarmament which they ensured deprived the German nation of all its rights, but far more so because of the consequent destruction of the material existence of one of the great civilised nations in the world, and the proposed annihilation of its future, the utterly senseless accumulation of immense tracts of territory under the domination of a number of states, the theft of all the irrepairable foundations of life and indispensable vital necessities from a conquered nation. While this dictate was being drawn up, men of insight even among our foes were uttering warnings about the terrible consequences which the ruthless application of its insane conditions would entail – a proof that even among them the conviction predominated that such a dictate could not possibly be held up in days to come. Their objections and protests were silenced by the assurance that the statutes of the newly created League of Nations provided for a revision of these conditions; in fact, the League was supposed to be the competent authority. The hope of revision was thus at no time regarded as presumptuous, but as something natural. Unfortunately, the Geneva institution, as those responsible for Versailles had intended, never looked upon itself as a body competent to undertake any sensible revision, but from the very outset as nothing more than the guarantor of the ruthless enforcement and maintenance of the conditions imposed at Versailles.

All attempts made by democratic Germany to obtain equality for the German people by a revision of the Treaty proved unavailing . . .

It is always in the interests of a conqueror to represent stipulations that are to his advantage as sacrosanct, while the instinct of self-preservation in the vanquished leads him to reacquire the common human rights that he has lost. For him, the dictate of an overbearing conqueror had all the less legal force, since he had never been honourably conquered. Owing to a rare misfortune, the German Empire, between 1914 and 1918, lacked good leadership. To this, and to the as yet unenlightened faith and trust placed by the German people in the words of democratic statesmen, our downfall was due.

Hence the Franco-British claim that the Dictate of Versailles was a sort of international, or even a supreme, code of laws, appeared to be nothing more than a piece of insolent arrogance to every honest German, the assumption, however, that British or French statesmen should actually claim to be the guardians of justice, and even of human culture, as mere effrontery. A piece of effrontery that is thrown into a sufficiently glaring light by their own extremely negligible achievements in this direction. For seldom have any countries in the world been ruled with a lesser degree of wisdom, morality and culture than those which are at the moment exposed to the ragings of certain democratic statesmen.

The programme of the National Socialist Movement, besides freeing the Reich from the innermost fetters of a small substratum of Jewish-capitalist and pluto-democratic profiteers, proclaimed to the world our resolution to shake off the shackles of the Versailles Dictate.

"THE SPECTRE OF COMMUNISM"
Karl Marx

The preamble, below, to *The Communist Manifesto* is a general
statement of intent (this version is from the 1888 English
edition) of the newly formed Communist Party. It compares
Communism to a spectre in order to point out that leaders are
decrying the movement without understanding it. The manifesto
itself is divided into sections: Bourgeois and Prolitarians;
Prolitarians and Communists; Socialist and Communist
Literature; and Position of the Communists in Relation to the
Various Existing Opposition Parties. The second part contained
the 'ten planks', which included the abolition of property and
giving of rents of land to public purposes; heavy progressive
income tax; abolition of rights of inheritance; confiscation of
the property of emigrants and rebels; centralization of credit
in the hands of the state; centralization of communication
and transport in the hands of the State; extension of public
ownership of factories and farms; equal liability to work and
the establishment of industrial and agricultural armies; and free
education for all children and abolition of child labour in favour
of a combination of education and industrial production.

A spectre is haunting Europe – the spectre of Communism. All the
Powers of old Europe have entered into a holy alliance to exorcise
this spectre: Pope and Czar, Metternich and Guizot, French
Radicals and German police-spies.

Where is the party in opposition that has not been decried as
Communistic by its opponents in power? Where is the Opposition
that has not hurled back the branding reproach of Communism,
against the more advanced opposition parties, as well as against its
reactionary adversaries?

Two things result from this fact.

I. Communism is already acknowledged by all European Powers

to be itself a Power.

II. It is high time that Communists should openly, in the face of the whole world, publish their views, their aims, their tendencies, and meet this nursery tale of the Spectre of Communism with a Manifesto of the party itself.

"CLOSING HIS MILITARY SERVICE"
Douglas MacArthur

In 1949, General MacArthur handed control of Japan to the new government but remained in the east until 1951, when President Truman dismissed him from his command after he had publicly queried the administration's policy of limiting the Korean War in order to avoid a wider conflict with China and the involvement of the Soviet Union, which by now possessed nuclear weapons. The general gave a farewell address to Congress, during which he stated his belief that criticism of him among people who did not understand warfare or the threat that communist China posed had distorted his position and led to his being labelled a warmonger, whereas in fact as a soldier with more than 50 years' experience, he loathed war and felt it a useless way to end international disputes. He ended his address:

I am closing my 52 years of military service. When I joined the army, even before the turn of the century, it was the fulfillment of all my boyish hopes and dreams.

The world has turned over many times since I took the oath on the plain at West Point, and the hopes and dreams have long since vanished, but I still remember the refrain of one of the most popular barracks ballads of that day which proclaimed most proudly that old soldiers never die; they just fade away.

And like the old soldier of that ballad, I now close my military career and just fade away, an old soldier who tried to do his duty as God gave him the light to see that duty. Goodbye.

"A SLEEPING ENEMY"
Isoroku Yamamoto

After the attacks on Pearl Harbor and other allied sites in December 1941, the Commander-in-Chief of the Combined Fleet, Admiral Isoroku Yamamoto, made the comment below in an interview for the daily newspaper *Asahi Shimbun*. Even before the attack, he had realised that he would have to destroy the US Pacific Fleet completely in order for the pre-emptive strike to work. Because that aim was not achieved – and because of the issue of the timing of the attack – he knew that he had succeeded in doing just what he did not want. He knew, too, that the American military had a far greater capacity than Japan's to re-arm and redeploy ships and aircraft and had earlier said that he would be able to win victory after victory for the first few months, but if war carried on longer than that, he could not predict the outcome.

A military man can scarcely pride himself on having 'smitten a sleeping enemy'; it is more a matter of shame, simply, for the one smitten. I would rather you made your appraisal after seeing what the enemy does, since it is certain that, angered and outraged, he will soon launch a determined counterattack.

"THE SUBLIME TO THE RIDICULOUS"
Napoleon Bonaparte

Napoleon's 1812 attack on Russia, culminating in the Battle of Borodino on 7 September, marked both the greatest extent of Napoleon's empire and the beginning of its downfall. Rather than surrender the city, the Russians had evacuated it and set fire to it and the Tsar did not surrender. About a month later, with unrest at home and the prospect of a harsh Russian winter, Napoleon turned for home, leaving the army to follow. Fewer than 40,000 of the 450,000 personnel he had set out with made it out of Russia because of continued Russian military action, the winter weather and the murder of stragglers by vengeful peasants. At the Beresina river alone, he lost 35,000 men. In December, before his full losses were apparent, he made the following remark to the Polish Ambassador, Abbé de Pradt.

Du sublime au ridicule il n'y a qu'un pas. (From the sublime to the ridiculous there is but one step.)

"I HATE WAR"
Franklin D. Roosevelt

During the Presidential election campaign of 1936, President Roosevelt toured widely, and in August returned to one of his favourite stomping grounds, Chautauqua. In a speech that defined his foreign policy for most of his second term, the need for peaceful relations with other countries, including his 'good-neighbor' policy with regard to the countries to the south, and neutrality for countries farther away. The 'weapons' he describes as having been given to him by Congress are the first Neutrality Acts, which enabled him to embargo the sales of armaments to 'belligerent' nations and in some cases travel to them.

As many of you who are here tonight know, I formed the excellent habit of coming to Chautauqua more than 20 years ago. After my inauguration in 1933, I promised Mr Bestor that during the next four years I would come to Chautauqua again; it is in fulfillment of this that I am with you tonight.

A few days ago I was asked what the subject of this talk would be, and I replied that for two good reasons I wanted to discuss the subject of peace. First, because it is eminently appropriate in Chautauqua; and, secondly, because in the hurly-burly of domestic politics it is important that our people should not overlook problems and issues which, though they lie beyond our borders, may, and probably will, have a vital influence on the United States of the future.

I say this to you not as a confirmed pessimist but as one who still hopes that envy, hatred, and malice among nations have reached their peak and will be succeeded by a new tide of peace and good will. I say this as one who has participated in many of the decisions of peace and war before, during, and after the World War; one who has traveled much, and one who has spent a goodly portion of every 24 hours in the study of foreign relations.

Long before I returned to Washington as President of the United States I had made up my mind that, pending what might be called a more opportune moment on other continents, the United States could best serve the cause of a peaceful humanity by setting an example. That was why on March 4, 1933, I made the following declaration.

'In the field of world policy I would dedicate this nation to the policy of the good neighbor – the neighbor who resolutely respects himself and, because he does so, respects the rights of others – the neighbor who respects his obligations and respects the sanctity of his agreements in and with a world of neighbors.'

This declaration represents my purpose; but it represents more than a purpose, for it stands for a practice . . . the whole world now knows that the United States cherishes no predatory ambitions. We are strong; but less powerful nations know that they need not fear our strength. We seek no conquest: we stand for peace.

In the whole of the western hemisphere our good-neighbor policy has produced results that are especially heartening.

The noblest monument to peace and to neighborly economic and social friendship in all the world is not a monument in bronze or stone, but the boundary which unites the United States and Canada – 3,000 miles of friendship with no barbed wire, no gun or soldier, and no passport on the whole frontier.

Mutual trust made that frontier. To extend the same sort of mutual trust throughout the Americas was our aim.

The American republics to the south of us have been ready always to cooperate with the United States on a basis of equality and mutual respect, but before we inaugurated the good-neighbor policy there was among them resentment and fear because certain administrations in Washington had slighted their national pride and their sovereign rights . . .

Peace, like charity, begins at home; that is why we have begun at home. But peace in the western world is not all that we seek.

It is our hope that knowledge of the practical application of the good-neighbor policy in this hemisphere will be borne home to our neighbors across the seas. For ourselves we are on good terms with them – terms in most cases of straightforward friendship, of peaceful understanding.

But, of necessity, we are deeply concerned about tendencies of recent years among many of the nations of other continents. It is a bitter experience to us when the spirit of agreements to which we are a party is not lived up to. It is an even more bitter experience for the whole company of nations to witness not only the spirit but the letter of international agreements violated with impunity and without regard to the simple principles of honor. Permanent friendships between nations as between men can be sustained only by scrupulous respect for the pledged word . . .

We are not isolationists except insofar as we seek to isolate ourselves completely from war. Yet we must remember that so long as war exists on Earth there will be some danger that even the nation which most ardently desires peace may be drawn into war.

I have seen war. I have seen war on land and sea. I have seen blood running from the wounded. I have seen men coughing out their gassed lungs. I have seen the dead in the mud. I have seen cities destroyed. I have seen two hundred limping, exhausted men come out of line—the survivors of a regiment of one thousand that went forward forty-eight hours before. I have seen children starving. I have seen the agony of mothers and wives. I hate war . . .

I wish I could keep war from all nations, but that is beyond my power. I can at least make certain that no act of the United States helps to produce or to promote war. I can at least make clear that the conscience of America revolts against war and that any nation which provokes war forfeits the sympathy of the people of the United States . . .

In one field, that of economic barriers, the American policy may be, I hope, of some assistance in discouraging the economic source of war and therefore a contribution toward the peace of the world. The trade agreements which we are making are not only finding outlets for the products of American fields and American factories but are also pointing the way to the elimination of embargoes, quotas, and other devices which place such pressure on nations not possessing great natural resources that to them the price of peace seems less terrible than the price of war.

The Congress of the United States has given me certain authority to provide safeguards of American neutrality in case of war.

The President of the United States who, under our Constitution, is vested with primary authority to conduct our international relations, thus has been given new weapons with which to maintain our neutrality.

Nevertheless – and I speak from a long experience – the effective maintenance of American neutrality depends today, as in the past, on the wisdom and determination of whoever at the moment occupy the offices of President and Secretary of State . . .

We seek to dominate no other nation. We ask no territorial expansion. We oppose imperialism. We desire reduction in world armaments.

We believe in democracy; we believe in freedom; we believe in peace. We offer to every nation of the world the handclasp of good neighbor. Let those who wish our friendship look us in eye and take our hand.

"HITLER'S ARMY CAN BE DEFEATED"
Joseph Stalin

In June 1941, Germany broke the non-aggression pact of 1939 and invaded the Soviet Union in the attack code-named Operation Barbarossa. Stalin was taken by surprise because although he knew that German troops were massing on the eastern borders, he had not expected an attack until after Hitler's planned conquest of the UK. On 2 July, in a radio broadcast to the nation, the opening of which is below, he denounced the Germans and urged the people to devote all their efforts to the defeat of the enemy.

Comrades! Citizens!

The perfidious military attack by Hitler's Germany on our motherland, begun on June 22, is continuing. In spite of the heroic resistance of the Red Army and although the enemy's finest divisions and finest air units have already been shattered and have met their doom on the battlefield, the enemy continues to push forward, hurling fresh forces into the fray . . .

. . . History shows that there are no invincible armies and that there never have been. Napoleon's army was considered invincible, but it was beaten successively by the troops of Russia, England and Germany. Kaiser Wilhelm's German army in the period of the first imperialist war was also considered an invincible army, but it was defeated several times by Russian and Anglo-French troops, and was finally routed by the Anglo-French troops. The same must be said of Hitler's German fascist army today. This army has not yet met with serious resistance on the continent of Europe. Only on our territory has it met with serious resistance. And if as a result of this the finest divisions of the German fascist army have been defeated by our Red Army, it shows that Hitler's fascist army can also be and will be defeated as were the armies of Napoleon and Wilhelm.

"THE BATTLE OF FRANCE IS OVER . . ."
Winston Churchill

Two weeks after the evacuation of British troops from Dunkirk on 18 June, 1940 there were still about 50,000 members of the British Expeditionary Force fighting in France alongside the French Army. However, defeat in the Battle of France was by now almost inevitable and troops were being pulled back. The French would have to seek terms for surrender a week later and with France in German hands, the British Isles would be under direct threat. Churchill outlined to the House of Commons why and how he was convinced that the army, navy and air force would be able to repel invasion and concluded:

What General Weygand called the Battle of France is over. I expect that the Battle of Britain is about to begin. Upon this battle depends the survival of Christian civilization. Upon it depends our own British life, and the long continuity of our institutions and our Empire. The whole fury and might of the enemy must very soon be turned on us. Hitler knows that he will have to break us in this Island or lose the war. If we can stand up to him, all Europe may be free and the life of the world may move forward into broad, sunlit uplands. But if we fail, then the whole world, including the United States, including all that we have known and cared for, will sink into the abyss of a new Dark Age made more sinister, and perhaps more protracted, by the lights of perverted science. Let us therefore brace ourselves to our duties, and so bear ourselves that, if the British Empire and its Commonwealth last for a thousand years, men will still say, 'This was their finest hour.'.

"TO PREVENT WAR AND PREPARE FOR WAR"
Albert Einstein

Before the dropping of the atom bomb on Hiroshima, Einstein had predicted that such devices would have horrendous effects. He is reported to have been so distraught that his work had contributed to such a terrible force for destruction that he expressed a wish to have been a watchmaker (or a plumber, or any of various other artisan professions). In an address at a symposium in Princeton the following year – The Social Task of the Scientist in the Atomic Era – he discussed his vision of a paradoxical future in a world where war must be prevented, but in order to do so, everyone must prepare for war.

The position in which we are now is a very strange one which in general political life never happened. Namely, the thing that I refer to is this: To have security against atomic bombs and against the other biological weapons, we have to prevent war, for if we cannot prevent war every nation will use every means that is at their disposal; and in spite of all promises they make, they will do it. At the same time, so long as war is not prevented, all the governments of the nations have to prepare for war, and if you have to prepare for war, then you are in a state where you cannot abolish war.

This is really the cornerstone of our situation. Now, I believe what we should try to bring about is the general conviction that the first thing you have to abolish is war at all costs, and every other point of view must be of secondary importance.

"MAJOR COMBAT OPERATIONS IN IRAQ HAVE ENDED"
George W. Bush

Standing on the deck of USS *Abraham Lincoln*, in front of a banner proclaiming 'Mission Accomplished' President Bush addressed a crowd of military personnel. He started by saying that the major combat operations in Iraq were over and that work would now be directed towards reconstruction and the setting up of a new democratic government. He also repeated warnings that any terrorist who sought to harm America or its allies would bear the consequences. His assessment that operations in Iraq were by no means over and that insurgency would be a continuing problem have proved only too right, but the assertion that Saddam Hussein's regime was supporting Al Qaeda has since been discounted by most authorities.

. . . my fellow Americans, major combat operations in Iraq have ended. In the battle of Iraq, the United States and our allies have prevailed.

And now our coalition is engaged in securing and reconstructing that country.

In this battle, we have fought for the cause of liberty and for the peace of the world. Our nation and our coalition are proud of this accomplishment, yet it is you, the members of the United States military, who achieved it. Your courage, your willingness to face danger for your country and for each other made this day possible. Because of you our nation is more secure. Because of you the tyrant has fallen and Iraq is free . . .

This nation thanks all of the members of our coalition who joined in a noble cause. We thank the armed forces of the United Kingdom, Australia and Poland who shared in the hardships of war. We thank all of the citizens of Iraq who welcomed our troops and joined in the liberation of their own country.

And tonight, I have a special word for Secretary Rumsfeld, for General Franks and for all the men and women who wear the uniform of the United States: America is grateful for a job well done.

With new tactics and precision weapons, we can achieve military objectives without directing violence against civilians.

No device of man can remove the tragedy from war, yet it is a great advance when the guilty have far more to fear from war than the innocent.

In the images of celebrating Iraqis we have also seen the ageless appeal of human freedom. Decades of lies and intimidation could not make the Iraqi people love their oppressors or desire their own enslavement.

Men and women in every culture need liberty like they need food and water and air. Everywhere that freedom arrives, humanity rejoices and everywhere that freedom stirs, let tyrants fear.

We have difficult work to do in Iraq. We're bringing order to parts of that country that remain dangerous. We're pursuing and finding leaders of the old regime who will be held to account for their crimes. We've begun the search for hidden chemical and biological weapons, and already know of hundreds of sites that will be investigated . . .

The transition from dictatorship to democracy will take time, but it is worth every effort. Our coalition will stay until our work is done and then we will leave and we will leave behind a free Iraq.

The battle of Iraq is one victory in a war on terror that began on September the 11th, 2001 and still goes on . . .

The liberation of Iraq is a crucial advance in the campaign against terror. We have removed an ally of al-Qaeda and cut off a source of terrorist funding . . .

And wherever you go, you carry a message of hope, a message that is ancient and ever new. In the words of the prophet Isaiah, 'To the captives, come out; and to those in darkness, be free.'.

Thank you for serving our country and our cause.

May God bless you all. And may God continue to bless America.

"REMEMBERING KOSOVO HEROISM"
Slobodan Milosevic

On 28 June, 1989 Serb President Milosovic gave a speech at the
monument to the battle of Kosovo. Since 1974, Kosovo had
been an autonomous region within Yugoslavia populated
mainly by ethnic Albanians, but to the Serbs it remained their
spiritual homeland. Demands for greater Kosovan autonomy
and discrimination against Serbs and Montenegrins there led
Milosovic to institute a repressive constitution. His speech at
the heart of Kosovo three months after the suppression of riots
was a reassertion of Serbian control and a forewarning, as
Yugoslavia fell apart in the worst violence in Europe since the
end of World War II.

By the force of social circumstances this great 600th anniversary of
the Battle of Kosovo is taking place in a year in which Serbia, after
many years, after many decades, has regained its state, national,
and spiritual integrity. Therefore, it is not difficult for us to answer
today the old question: how are we going to face Milos? Through
the play of history and life, it seems as if Serbia has, precisely in
this year, in 1989, regained its state and its dignity and thus has
celebrated an event of the distant past which has a great historical
and symbolic significance . . .

The lack of unity and betrayal in Kosovo will continue to follow
the Serbian people like an evil fate through the whole of its history.
Even in the last war, this lack of unity and betrayal led the Serbian
people and Serbia into agony, the consequences of which in the
historical and moral sense exceeded fascist aggression . . .

Let the memory of Kosovo heroism live forever!

Long live Serbia!

Long live Yugoslavia!

Long live peace and brotherhood among peoples!

Miscellaneous

"HAMLET: ACT 3, SCENE 1"
William Shakespeare

Possibly the most eloquent suicide threat ever, this soliloquy is
the turning point in *Hamlet*, marking the beginning of the play's
descent into madness and violence. Hamlet's feigned lunacy later
in the scene prefigures Ophelia's real insanity and his rage in a
tragedy that soon sees most of the protagonists dead. The play is
thought to mirror the political situation in England at the time,
towards the end of Queen Elizabeth I's life, but opinions differ
as to whether the characters are meant to be counterparts to
real people. Could the gloomy legitimate heir Hamlet represent
James VI of Scotland or might that be Fortinbras, the king
waiting just over the border to invade?

To be, or not to be: that is the question:
Whether 'tis nobler in the mind to suffer
The slings and arrows of outrageous fortune,
Or to take arms against a sea of troubles,
And by opposing end them? To die: to sleep;
No more; and by a sleep to say we end
The heart-ache and the thousand natural shocks
That flesh is heir to, 'tis a consummation

Devoutly to be wish'd. To die, to sleep;
To sleep: perchance to dream: ay, there's the rub;
For in that sleep of death what dreams may come
When we have shuffled off this mortal coil,
Must give us pause: there's the respect
That makes calamity of so long life;
For who would bear the whips and scorns of time,
The oppressor's wrong, the proud man's contumely,
The pangs of despised love, the law's delay,
The insolence of office and the spurns
That patient merit of the unworthy takes,
When he himself might his quietus make
With a bare bodkin? Who would fardels bear,
To grunt and sweat under a weary life,
But that the dread of something after death,
The undiscover'd country from whose bourn
No traveller returns, puzzles the will
And makes us rather bear those ills we have
Than fly to others that we know not of?
Thus conscience does make cowards of us all;
And thus the native hue of resolution
Is sicklied o'er with the pale cast of thought,
And enterprises of great pitch and moment
With this regard their currents turn awry,
And lose the name of action.

"BIG BROTHER"
George Orwell

Orwell was a writer and journalist, a veteran of the fight against fascism in the Spanish Civil War. He loathed totalitarianism and was passionate about social injustice. His two most famous novels, *Animal Farm* and *1984*, are both critiques of political systems, although in other works he would lampoon middle-class morés. The main slogan used in *1984* to keep the oppressed population under control, reproduced below, has passed into such common currency (and television folklore) that many people who use it may not even realize its source.

Big Brother is watching you.

"MARCONI GENERAL SENDS DISTRESS CALL"
RMS *Titanic* (and various other vessels)

During the night of 14–15 April, 1912 the supposedly unsinkable ship RMS *Titanic* hit an iceberg far south of where any would be expected at that time of year. Within little over two-and-a-half hours she had sunk, taking 1,517 people with her. Due to the rapid timescale, only 711 of the 2,223 people on board made it to lifeboats. The two Marconi wireless operators, Jack Phillips and Harold Bride, worked tirelessly until the power supply to the radios gave out just after 2.00 am. RMS *Carpathia* picked up the first survivors from the lifeboats some time after 6.00 am.

00.15 *Titanic*
CQD (6 times) DE MGY [6 times] position 41.44 N. 50.24 W . . . (repeated over and again)

00.18 *Carpathia* (to *Titanic*)
Do you know that Cape Cod is sending a batch of messages for you?

Titanic (to *Carpathia*)
Come at once. We have struck a berg. It's a CQD OM (it's a distress situation old man) Position 41.46 N. 50.14 W.

Carpathia (to *Titanic*)
Shall I tell my Captain? Do you require assistance?

Titanic (to *Carpathia*)
Yes, come quick.

00.25 *Titanic* (to *Ypiranga* about 15–20 times)
CQD, Here corrected position 41.46 N. 50.14 W.
Require immediate assistance. We have collision with iceberg.

Sinking. Can hear nothing for noise of steam.

00.26 *Prinz Friedrich Wilhelm* (to *Titanic*)
Titanic my position at 12 am 39.47 N. 50.10 W.

Titanic (to *Prinz Friedrich Wilhelm*)
Are you coming to our (. . .) We have collision with iceberg.
Sinking. Please tell Captain to come.

Prinz Friedrich Wilhelm (to *Titanic*)
OK will tell.

00.27 *Titanic*
I require assistance immediately. Struck by iceberg in 41.46 N.
50.14 W.

00. 34 *Frankfurt* (to *Titanic*)
My position 39.47 N. 52.10 W.

Titanic (to *Frankfurt*)
Are you coming to our assistance?

Frankfurt (to *Titanic*)
What is the matter with you?

Titanic (to *Frankfurt*)
We have struck an iceberg and sinking. Please tell Captain to come.

Frankfurt (to *Titanic*)
OK. Will tell the bridge right away.

Titanic (to *Frankfurt*)
OK, yes, quick.

00.45 *Titanic* (to *Olympic*)
SOS.

00.50 *Titanic*

CQD I require immediate assistance. Position 41.46 N. 50.14 W.

01.00 *Titanic*
CQD I require immediate assistance. Position 41.46 N. 50.14 W.

Titanic (to *Olympic*)
My position is 41.46 N. 50.14 W. We have struck an iceberg.

01.10 *Titanic* (to *Olympic*)
We are in collision with berg. Sinking head down. 41.46 N. 50.14 W. Come soon as possible.

01.10 *Titanic* (to *Olympic*)
Captain says Get your boats ready. What is your position?

01.15 *Baltic* (to *Caronia*)
Please tell *Titanic* we are making towards her.

01.20 *Cape Race* (to *Titanic*)
We are coming to your assistance. Our position 170 miles N. of you.

01.25 *Caronia* (to *Titanic*)
Baltic coming to your assistance.

Olympic (to *Titanic*)
Position 4.24 am GMT 40.52 N. 61.18 W. Are you steering southerly to meet us?

01.30 *Titanic* (to *Olympic*)
We are putting passengers off in small boats. Women and children in boats, cannot last much longer.

01.35 *Olympic* (to *Titanic*)
What weather do you have?

Titanic (to *Olympic*)
Clear and calm.

"THE DEATH OF PRINCESS DIANA"
BBC radio

The news that the Princess of Wales had been badly hurt in a car accident in Paris had broken on the British media at about 1:15 on Sunday August 31, 1997. Rumours started flying round that ranged from Diana had been seen walking away from the accident to her dying at the scene. The confirmation of her death was released first on BBC radio at 5:20 and on the television just before 6 am. The mass display of public grief took the British establishment by surprise.

This is BBC Radio. Buckingham Palace has confirmed the death of Diana, Princess of Wales. In a statement it said that the Queen and Prince Philip were deeply shocked and distressed by this terrible news. Other members of the Royal Family are being informed of the Princess's death.

"EARTHQUAKE WARNING"
Pacific Tsunami Warning Center

Eight minutes after almost 1,000 miles of the ocean floor surface sprang up by about 50 feet, the seismic waves reached the Pacific Tsunami Warning Center in Hawaii. Seven minutes later, staff issued the advisory below by telephone, text and other methods to the effect that there was little risk of a tsunami in the Pacific. Another bulletin issued 50 minutes later mentioned the possibility of a tsunami near the earthquake's epicentre. A minute later, the first waves struck Northern Sumatra and the Nicobar Islands. The tsunami killed more than 225,000 people, in countries as far away as Somalia. As a result of the tsunami – and the deaths that resulted from the lack of any method of detection or warning of tsunamis in the region – a network of detectors has now been deployed.

TSUNAMI BULLETIN NUMBER 001
PACIFIC TSUNAMI WARNING
CENTER/NOAA/NWS
ISSUED AT 0114Z 26 DEC 2004

THIS BULLETIN IS FOR ALL AREAS OF THE PACIFIC BASIN EXCEPT ALASKA – BRITISH COLUMBIA – WASHINGTON – OREGON – CALIFORNIA.

. . . TSUNAMI INFORMATION BULLETIN . . .

THIS MESSAGE IS FOR INFORMATION ONLY. THERE IS NO TSUNAMI WARNING OR WATCH IN EFFECT.

AN EARTHQUAKE HAS OCCURRED WITH THESE PRELIMINARY PARAMETERS

ORIGIN TIME – 0059Z 26 DEC 2004
COORDINATES – 3.4 NORTH 95.7 EAST
LOCATION – OFF W COAST OF NORTHERN SUMATERA
MAGNITUDE – 8.0

EVALUATION

THIS EARTHQUAKE IS LOCATED OUTSIDE THE PACIFIC.
NO DESTRUCTIVE TSUNAMI THREAT EXISTS BASED ON
HISTORICAL EARTHQUAKE AND TSUNAMI DATA.

THIS WILL BE THE ONLY BULLETIN ISSUED FOR THIS
EVENT UNLESS ADDITIONAL INFORMATION BECOMES
AVAILABLE.

THE WEST COAST/ALASKA TSUNAMI WARNING CENTER
WILL ISSUE BULLETINS FOR ALASKA – BRITISH COLUMBIA –
WASHINGTON – OREGON – CALIFORNIA.

"EVERYBODY WILL BE FAMOUS"
Andy Warhol

A successful commercial artist in the 1950s, Andy Warhol shot to fame in the 1960s as a leader in the field of Pop Art, with works featuring such items as Campbell's soup cans and Brillo pads, plus the series of prints featuring repeated images of Marylin Monroe in an assortment of lurid colours. From 1965 he collaborated with singer-songwriter Lou Reed and managed the Velvet Underground. He surrounded himself with an entourage of bohemian artists and personalities who would appear in his Factory films and used to accompany him in large numbers to the best-known clubs in New York, one of which – Studio 54 – he later described as being the place where his famous prediction actually came true.

In the future, everybody will be world famous for 15 minutes.

INDEX OF SPEAKERS

ACKNOWLEDGEMENTS

Menachem Begin – © The State of Israel; Buddha's Fire Sermon – translated by Nanamoli Thera © Buddhist Publication Society; George W/ Bush – courtesy George W. Bush Presidential Library and Museum; Albert Einstein – © Institute for Advanced Studies, Philadelphia and © Albert Einstein for the Emergency Committee of Atomic Scientists, Inc.; Dwight D. Eisenhower – courtesy Dwight D. Eisenhower Presidential Library; Ho Chi Minh – Selected Works, courtesy of the Foreign Languages Publishing House, Hanoi; Jesse Jackson – © Rev. Jesse Jackson, Snr; John F. Kennedy – courtesy of John F. Kennedy Presidential Library and Museum; Barack Obama – courtesy www.whitehouse.gov; Ronald Reagan – courtesy of Ronald Reagan Presidential Library; Franklin D. Roosevelt – courtesy of Franklin D. Roosevelt Presidential Library and Museum; Margaret Thatcher – © The Margaret Thatcher Foundation.